AT THE PLEASURE OF HIS

MAJESTY

Chander M. Lall is a designated senior advocate practising law largely in the Delhi High Court and the Supreme Court of India. He founded the law firm Lall & Sethi in 1994, of which he was the managing partner till 2017. He has contributed as a writer to many publications, including *Trademark Law and the Internet* and *Trademark Anti-Counterfeiting in the Asia-Pacific* published by the International Trademark Association. He is considered an authority on intellectual property law and has been lead counsel in many groundbreaking decisions on the subject.

The author is a cyclist and an outdoor enthusiast, engaging frequently in skiing, surfing, scuba diving, kayaking, rafting, mountaineering and rock climbing. He is a keen collector of artefacts and a naturalist at heart.

AT THE PLEASURE OF HIS

MAJESTY

I.M. LALL AND THE CASE THAT SHOOK THE CROWN

CHANDER M. LALL

RUPA

Published by
Rupa Publications India Pvt. Ltd 2024
7/16, Ansari Road, Daryaganj
New Delhi 110002

Sales centres:
Bengaluru Chennai
Hyderabad Jaipur Kathmandu
Kolkata Mumbai Prayagraj

Copyright © Chander M. Lall 2024

The views and opinions expressed in this book are the author's own and the facts are as reported by him which have been verified to the extent possible, and the publishers are not in any way liable for the same.

All rights reserved.
No part of this publication may be reproduced, transmitted, or stored in a retrieval system, in any form or by any means, electronic, mechanical, photocopying, recording or otherwise, without the prior permission of the publisher.

P-ISBN: 978-93-5702-751-9
E-ISBN: 978-93-5702-833-2

First impression 2024

10 9 8 7 6 5 4 3 2 1

The moral right of the author has been asserted.

Printed in India

This book is sold subject to the condition that it shall not, by way of trade or otherwise, be lent, resold, hired out, or otherwise circulated, without the publisher's prior consent, in any form of binding or cover other than that in which it is published.

This book is dedicated to my late father, Amar Raj Lall (Bar-at-Law), whose graphic narratives motivated me to write this book. The book is also dedicated to my grandfather, Inder Mohan Lall (ICS). I have been informed through reliable sources that I was his favourite grandchild.

Here's to you, Pa and Grand Pa.

You both will remain the heroes of my life...forever.

Contents

Foreword

Not many know the origins of Article 311 of the Constitution of India, which is the bedrock on which the civil services in India stand. Every lawyer of repute has argued in favour of many government servants in their disputes with the government, both at the Centre and in the states. It was nothing short of a revelation to me when I learnt that the most precious right contained in the Article 311 is owed almost entirely to the labours of one man, Inder Mohan Lall, the grandfather of the author, who, in his own right, is a leading lawyer practising in New Delhi.

Inder Mohan Lall's family hailed from Mianwali, a small town near Lahore, now in Pakistan. The early chapters of the book narrate how a young boy, fired by ambition, found his way to Lahore, got himself a college degree and a law degree, got enlisted in the British Indian Army, fought in Mesopotamia during the First World War, travelled to London to be interviewed for the ICS and secured an appointment on the judicial side.

When Inder Mohan was serving as the district and sessions judge in Multan and Peshawar, he ran into trouble with the British government, was charge-sheeted and ultimately dismissed from service. Between June 1940 and March 1948, Inder Mohan took on the British government and fought his case through three courts—the High Court, the Federal Court and the Privy Council. He won in all three courts, and the law was declared that a civil servant must be told the grounds on which action against him has been proposed and that he must be given an opportunity to show cause against the proposed punishment. Since the procedure was not followed in this case, the order of dismissal was set aside, and it was declared that Inder Mohan remained a member of the ICS.

This story alone would have been sufficient for a good book, especially for lawyers, but the author has told many other stories too. One that is heart-wrenching talks about the horrors that accompanied Partition. There is another story about the real-life adventures of the author's father, Amar, who made several trips after Partition, in and out of Pakistan, to retrieve the family's belongings, including the Studebaker car and loads of Kraft cheese!

Altogether, this book is a pleasant read on a Saturday afternoon—which is what I did—and leaves the reader with an intriguing mix of sadness and happiness.

–P. Chidambaram
Member of Parliament, Rajya Sabha

Tea party organized to bid farewell to the outgoing claims officer and to meet I.M. Lall, ICS chief claims commissioner (sitting, third from left), on 4 September 1952, at Hotel Imperial
Source: Lall family albums

Introduction

Footloose in Haridwar (2018)

After a tiring journey from Delhi, I reached Haridwar at noon. My cousin Nick from Los Angeles and Jogi, my *chacha* (uncle), accompanied me. We had arrived in Haridwar with a purpose: to immerse the ashes of Tilak, Nick's father, in the Ganges. Although the Ganges may not have lured him during his lifetime, Tilak had requested that his ashes be brought to India and be immersed in Mother Ganga. Nick had come to fulfil his father's last wish, his last invocation.

Standing on one shore of the river, I saw a splash of colour on the opposite bank of the famous Har Ki Pauri or footsteps of god. Thousands of devotees and *sadhus* walk down these steps for a holy dip to attain *moksha*—release from the cycle of birth and rebirth. Innumerable families have walked down these steps to immerse urns, containing ashes of deceased family members, with the belief that this will help the departed soul find its place at the feet of the lord. My visit coincided with the monsoon month of Shravan, and the famous Kanwar[1] pilgrimage was underway. Crowds of devotees had gathered to perform a centuries-old custom:

[1]The Kanwar pilgrimage is an annual pilgrimage undertaken by devotees of Shiva to Hindu pilgrimage places of Haridwar, Gaumukh and Gangotri in Uttarakhand, and Sultanganj in Bihar, to fetch holy waters of the Ganges.

collecting *Ganga jal* and carrying it barefoot to their villages, several hundred kilometres away.

To perform the last rites at the Asthi Pravah Ghat next to Har Ki Pauri, we proceeded to meet with our family pandit. From a very early age, my father, Amar, would often take me to Haridwar, particularly when there was a death in the family, to immerse the ashes of the departed into the Ganges. As soon as we would arrive, we would proceed to meet our family pandit and make an entry in the *bahi khata*[1] to update our family history. Back then, I was too young and uninterested to make a note of where we went. All I could recall was walking through narrow streets to reach the rather frugal home of our family pandit. The pandit would greet my father, assist in performing the last rites and eventually pull out the *bahi khata* containing the entries of our forefathers. I was told that our pandit had been able to trace entries for several generations before me. My father would pay the pandit handsomely in acknowledgement of his efforts, and we would be on our way back home. This was a significant source of the income for the pandits, and my father felt that unless they were paid well, the tradition would die.

My father had not accompanied me on this trip, and I was required to find the pandit myself. I had little idea of the locality and absolutely no idea of his name. When I asked around where I should look for the family pandit, I was pointed towards Kushavarta Ghat situated about 500 m down the river from Har Ki Pauri. We made our way through crowded markets reverberating with activity. When we reached our destination, we were greeted by many *pandas*. I told them

---

[1]The bahi khata, traditionally used for books of accounts, are long sheets of paper bound together from the top and folded in a red cloth.

that I was looking for my family pandit and they asked me for my *gotra* (lineage). I did not know about it, but I did know our surname at the time was Gera. Once that sequence was established, I was promptly taken to a residence that was familiar to me. It was the exact place I had visited many times with my father. I was informed that Purohit Chandan Prasad Kanta Prasad Jha was our family pandit, but he had passed away and the reins had been now handed to his son, Pandit Deepak Jha.

Pandit Deepak Jha lived in a small house. The front of the house was an empty room with a floor decorated with *chatais* (jute mats). Bahi khatas were stacked in one corner of the room. Jogi, Nick and I took off our footwear and entered this room. Pandit Deepak Jha, a young man, not more than 30 years old, greeted us and offered us hot chai, and asked if we were hungry. Pandit Deepak Jha was very different from the quintessential pandits of Haridwar. For one, he was very young. Being a panda at Haridwar was a family tradition, and he had inherited the bahi khatas from his father. He was now the repository of our family history. Like my father, I suddenly felt responsible to ensure that the tradition continued. Our first task was to perform the last rites of Tilak and thereafter update the bahi khatas and, in particular, enter the passing of Tilak. As Nick made his first entry in the bahi khata, we found that there was no indexing of these long sheets of bounded paper. Expert hands, such as those of Pandit Deepak Jha, would flip through pages, locating the appropriate entries. Each entry holds clues to previous entries. After all, these bahi khatas contain information about hundreds and thousands of families.

As we made ourselves comfortable in Pandit Jha's house, he started to take us through our lineage, a journey that was as riveting as it was emotionally charging. It was a reminder of the flow of life, each generation passing on the baton to the next. The room we were in came alive with memories of my ancestors. How many generations would have entered the very same doors and sat on the very same floor where we were sitting. The thought itself sent a shiver down my spine, but it was not an unpleasant feeling—it was recognition of being a part of something much bigger. My eyes turned moist as I read an entry in English written by my grandfather Inder Mohan's brother, Inder Bhan, who had come to Haridwar with the ashes of his father, Tahla Ram Gera, my great-grandfather. The entry read:

> I consigned the holy ashes of my beloved and respected father L. Tahla Ram Gera s/o L. Topan Ram Gera who breathed his last on 1st January 1937 according to 17th Posh 1993 at about 8:30 A.M. at his residential home at Mianwali at the age of 80 years approximately in the holy Ganges at Haridwar. My nephews Amar Raj Lall and Tilak Raj Lall were with me at the time of all the rites.

Amar Raj Lall, my father, was only nine years old at the time. His brother, Tilak, was three years older than him.

My grandfather, Inder Mohan Lall, would make regular visits to Haridwar. It was his travel destination of choice. This very passion for travel to Haridwar was also inherited by my father and to a lesser extent, by me. Every visit to the holy city also meant a visit to Pandit ji, as a result of which we secured a wealth of information from the bahi khata.

The trip not only helped me get acquainted with my lineage but also prompted me to look more closely at my family history. I grew up hearing stories of my grandfather, in particular, the famous case of the *High Commissioner for India and the High Commissioner for Pakistan vs I.M. Lall*[2], when he argued against the Crown in the Privy Council. This, after all, was the subcontinent's base case for service law jurisprudence. My father was a raconteur, and these stories formed a regular part of our diet. He also narrated other stories of how a small-town boy from Mianwali in present-day Pakistan made it to the heights of the ICS. I had the privilege of growing up listening to not only his and my grandfather's escapades but also his first-hand account of Partition.

As I sat there, soaking in the family history, my thoughts travelled to when I was a young boy, reading the 1976 novel *Roots: The Saga of an American Family*, wherein the American author Alex Haley traces his roots through a fictional character Kunta Kinte, a man from Gambia who was enslaved and taken to America in the eighteenth century. I decided to trace my roots through the protagonist, my grandfather, Inder Mohan, who, though not a fictional character, was the Kunta Kinte of my family, and I, perhaps, could play the role of the chronicler. That day, sitting in Pandit Jha's austere home, I decided to embark on the journey of unearthing my grandfather's rich life.

Since my grandfather was a government official in pre-Partition India, I started to look for archival records in India and in the United Kingdom (UK) where he fought his case. I came across documents and letters from my grandfather's days in service and decided to start noting all

---

[2]Reported as 1948 (Vol. LXXV) Privy Council 225; 'The High Commissioner for India ... vs I.M. Lall on 18 March, 1948', *Indian Kanoon*, https://indiankanoon.org/doc/1135972/. Accessed on 1 November 2023.

that I had heard and discovered. This book is the result of this endeavour.

This book recounts the hitherto untold story of how a small-town boy fulfilled his dreams by reaching a coveted post; how he courageously protected national treasures and held the conviction to single-handedly take on the British Empire. The story, interlaced with historical facts, shows how Inder Mohan was repeatedly pitted against powerful personalities, but his conviction and persistence made him victorious each time.

The book will be of interest to the legal fraternity, in particular those practising service law, as almost everybody will be familiar with the case discussed in the book. A further insight into how the case was fought against all odds would certainly interest legal practitioners. Additionally, those interested in history, Partition of India and the two World Wars will benefit from a first-hand account of what these wars meant for Indians and their families. Last but not the least, the book will appeal to all nationalists who take pride in being Indian. It celebrates yet another unsung hero who had the courage to take on the might of the Empire and emerge victorious, albeit at a huge cost of not just losing his job but also a young daughter, a home and the place he called his country.

—Chander M. Lall
New Delhi

1

From Geras to Lall—A Prism of the Past (1800-1913)

Inder Mohan was born as Inder Mohan Gera[1]. His father, Tahla Ram, was a moneylender in Mianwali. Back in 1901, the population of the town was approximately 3,591. Despite living in a largely agrarian society, education was given prime importance in the Gera household; children attended school and also performed household chores. Inder Mohan pumped water from the hand pump every day to fill the water troughs for the cattle. It was hard work, pumping water, carrying it in a steel bucket, pouring it into the trough, ensuring there was enough, so no animal went thirsty. Inder Mohan would go through the whole process multiple times a day.

Tired of the tediousness of this task, he concluded that there was no future for him in Mianwali. He packed his bags

---

[1]Gera also means 'peace' in Hindi. In Hebrew, 'Gera' means 'a grain' and is a common name for a man. In the Bible, it is a commonly used first name, including the name of Benjamin's son. Of course, it is also the name of a German city, but these are anecdotal facts. My ancestors, to the best of my knowledge, had no connection either with the Hebrew name or the German city. The Geras hail from a town called Mianwali, situated in the northwest of Pakistan, bordering Khyber-Pakhtunkhwa, and south of the Saraiki belt. Mianwali is located along the bank of river Indus bordering Bannu, Lakki Marwat in the west, Kohat and Karak in the northwest and Dera Ismail Khan in southwest.

and headed to Lahore, which was the closest educational destination to Mianwali. He must have been 17 years old at the time and already engaged to my grandmother, Dropadi, who was perhaps 10 years old. At the time, it was not unusual for close families to commit to marriages between their children at an early age. Dropadi's family, the Chawlas, lived close by in Mianwali itself.

I.M. Lall (standing second from left) with family in Mianwali
Source: Lall family albums

In Lahore, Inder Mohan got himself enrolled at the Government College University. He also changed his surname from 'Gera' to 'Lall'. For some reason, he felt 'Lall' (literal translation being 'red') suited his personality more than 'Gera' did. Significantly, the surname 'Gera' is derived from the word '*geru*', a red pigment used to colour earthen pots, to make them look new. The traditional Indian system of education—the *guru-shishya parampara*, wherein the Brahmins largely learnt about scriptures and religion, and the Kshatriyas about various aspects of warfare—had long been replaced by Islamic institutions of education, madrasas and *maktabs*. By the time he decided to pursue higher education, the British Raj was well entrenched in India, and education in English was considered the gold standard.

English education in India had started in the early 1820s through missionary schools. Later, through the English Education Act of 1835, the medium of instruction was changed from the Persian language to English. Thereafter, the British established a dense educational network with a Western curriculum in English. It was under this effort that the British established the Government College University Lahore (GCUL). By 1890, some 60,000 Indians passed the matriculation examination, chiefly in the liberal arts or law. About a third of those entered public administration, and another third became lawyers. The more ambitious upper-class men with money, which included luminaries, like Mohandas Karamchand Gandhi, Jawaharlal Nehru and Muhammed Ali Jinnah, went to England to obtain a legal education at the Inns of Court. Mahatma Gandhi had, in fact, pursued law at the University College London. He was trained at the Inner Temple and was called to the English Bar at the age of 22, in June 1891.

The GCUL was a historical institution. The British Raj originally sanctioned the establishment of a central college in Lahore in 1856, with teachers who claimed the University of Oxford, University of Cambridge, Dublin University and Durham University as their alma mater. Government College University Lahore, founded in 1861, was briefly affiliated with Brahma University under the leadership of Gottlieb Wilhelm Leitner, professor of Arabic and Islamic law at King's College

London, who was instrumental in laying the foundation of Panjab University in 1882. It was not until 1 January 1864 that the college opened its doors inside the palace of Raja Dhyan Singh, inside Lahore's walled city, where it operated as an affiliate college of Calcutta University. In April 1871, the college moved to a large bungalow near Anarkali Bazar in Lahore, and in 1873, its location was again changed—due to the rapidly increasing student strength—to another house called Rahim Khan's Kothi. Subsequently, in 1876, the college moved into its present building. Its first principal was Dr Leitner.

The prestige of the GCUL attracted Inder Mohan, and he completed his Bachelor of Arts from there. By then, the college had become a part of the Panjab University, one of the most prestigious universities of its time, established by the British government after convening the first meeting for establishing higher education institutions in October 1882 in Shimla.[2] The curriculum of the university and its colleges was Western, and the medium of instruction and learning was English—it would come in handy for Inder Mohan years later.

The Prestigious LLB Degree

Inder Mohan's pursuit of education did not end with a Bachelor's. He followed it up with a law degree, which had a unique significance in India at the time. Gandhi, a lawyer, had become a role model for Inder Mohan.

In the meantime, legal education in India was charting its own history. As the British Raj spread its roots in India, English

---

[2]Garrett, H.L.O., and Abdul Hamid, *A History of Government College Lahore*, Ripon Print Press, Lahore, 1964.

laws were spreading to all parts of the Empire. In India, between 1835 and 1855, a series of acts were passed along the lines of the new laws in England. These new laws were all recorded in English and, resultantly, it became necessary for the people to learn the language. The avowed object of legal education, at its very commencement, was to spread the knowledge of the laws, which could only be done through the learning of the English language. The purpose of legal education was to produce lower cadres of professional lawyers acquainted with English laws in the English language. At the outset, it was not feasible to lay down any minimum qualification—anyone who knew the English language well could study law and be qualified for the profession. If an Indian aspired to something higher and could afford to travel to England, he could join one of the Inns of Court in London.

The first formal university legal degree, the LLB (Legum Baccalaureus or Bachelor of Law) degree, began in Elphinstone College under the University of Bombay in 1860. To be eligible for the LLB degree course, one had to first become a graduate in Arts or Science. As the influence of the English language increased and the applicability of English laws gained prevalence in India, it required much more time to teach the same. Students keen to commence earning could ill afford this time. By 1909, the LLB degree course was reduced to two years after matriculation and a four-year degree course in Arts or Science.

This was the path followed by Inder Lall. Armed with matriculation and a legal degree, the next step for him was to sculpt his professional career. Who could have guessed that the First World War would form the plinth?

2

Inder: The God of War and the First World War (1914-18)

On 4 August 1914, Britain declared war on Germany, thus officially entering the First World War. The British government made an appeal to Indian leaders to support them in this time of crisis. The Indian leaders agreed, but they put their own terms and conditions, i.e., after the war was over, the British government would give constitutional (legislative and administrative) powers to the Indian people.

Indian troops entering Baghdad, in March 1917
Source: National Army Museum, London

Many Indians volunteered to join the army, as it not only offered a chance to break the caste system—with soldiers designated as *kshatriyas,* or the 'warrior' caste—but also because the soldiers were paid well. Of course, the added opportunity to participate in the administration of India, as promised by the British, was the icing on the cake.

An army recruitment poster calling for young men to get enlisted. The poster describes the monetary incentives that a soldier would get: ₹50 at the time of joining, an additional ₹15 to train during recruiting, a salary of ₹11 per month, ₹24 every six months after the completion of service. The monthly salary would be a sum of ₹15, and an additional ₹5 would be paid as field allowance during the war. The poster also mentions that soldiers would get good food and clothing for free.
Source: Imperial War Museums

Inder is the god of war. True to his name, Inder Mohan also enrolled himself in the British Indian Army. This, he thought, could be his opportunity to join the ICS. He had read in an advertisement issued by the British that those who were educated and were enlisting in the army would also get an opportunity to participate in the administration of British India, upon their return from the First World War. He was educated in the English language, was a matriculate and a lawyer, and therefore checked all the boxes.

The *Journal of the Society for Army Historical Research*, in an article, records how the First World War was the turning point in the deployment of Indian troops. Till then, Indian troops were used for dealing with internal problems. Now, with the need to deploy Indian troops in the world war, there was a need for extensive reforms in recruitment and training processes. Eurasians became liable for compulsory service. Indians were not conscripted, but efforts to attract them were redoubled. Recruiting boards were convened. Recruits were offered bonuses of a princely sum of ₹3. Salaries and pensions were increased, and rations were made free. Training became more 'systematic and intensive'. Colleges were established to prepare cadets for commissioning and training officers for field and staff rank. There were new schools to introduce the sepoy to modern warfare—artillery, machine-guns, hand grenades, driving and signalling.[1]

As initially the recruitments were based on incentives, the demand for soldiers multiplied manifold, resulting in more force being used in the recruitment process. Quota systems were introduced whereby the *zaildar*s (official in charge of a

---

[1]Cadell, Patrick, 'The Raising of the Indian Army', *Journal of the Society for Army Historical Research*, Vol. 34, No. 139, 1956, pp. 96–99.

zail, an administrative unit of a group of villages), *sufedposhes* (influential landlords or white collar gentry) and *lambardars* (revenue collectors) were required to raise a certain number of men through their influence or force. In 1918, Lieutenant Governor Michael O'Dwyer promised to raise as many as 200,000 men in the span of one year. Andrew Thompson, the chief secretary to the Punjab government, took a series of coercive measures; irrigation water supply was cut off and exorbitant revenues were levied on the zaildars who failed to meet the recruitment quota.[2]

The Mesopotamian Misadventure

Following Turkey's decision to enter the war on Germany's side, Britain sent troops to protect its oil supplies in the Ottoman province of Mesopotamia, a region located in the eastern Mediterranean, bound by the Zagros Mountains in the southeast and by the Arabian Plateau, corresponding to today's Iraq, Syria and Turkey. Control of the Persian Gulf was important for taking control of the seas and for a direct passage into India. The motivation of Britain was also to take dominant control over the Arab tribes and resultantly the region, giving them clear superiority over the Ottoman Empire.

The force sent to Mesopotamia constituted the largest British Indian Army contingent to serve abroad.[3] It was

[2]Banerjee, Poulumi, 'At First, Recruitment for the War Voluntary, But by 1918, the World War 1 Campaign Was Marked by Coercion', *Hindustan Times*, 11 November 2018, https://tinyurl.com/5dpurkz3. Accessed on 7 August 2023.

[3]By 1918, the Mesopotamian command was nearly half a million strong, a bulk of which were Indians.

christened the Indian Expeditionary Force D, under the command of Lt Gen. Sir John Nixon. The first unit, the 6th (Poona) Division, was sent in November 1914, serving initially under the command of Field Marshal Sir Arthur Arnold Barrett and then under Nixon. Inder Mohan was recruited as part of Indian Expeditionary Force D.

The Mesopotamian campaign had some early successes. The British army invaded Basra on 22 November 1914, opening the Iraqi front. The British troops under Gen. Charles Townsend then began their advance towards Baghdad. As the troops advanced, the General Commander of Iraq made a tactical retreat to the Ctesiphon area, approximately 30 km from Baghdad. The British troops took control of the town of Kut-al-Amara, 160 km south of Baghdad and on the left bank of the Tigris River, in September 1915, and set up their military base there. The Ottoman soldiers tactically evacuated Kut-al-Amara in December 1915, regrouped and counter-attacked the British who had taken control of the town with an 8,000-strong garrison. By the end of December 1915, the Ottomans surrounded the town, leaving the British and Indian soldiers with only limited supplies through the river route. Their ammunition and food soon ran out as the Ottomans tightened their grip around Kut.

The siege of Kut-al-Amara had begun on 7 December 1915 and ended on 29 April 1916, when the British garrison surrendered. The survivors of the siege were marched to imprisonment at Aleppo—4,000 British and Indian troops died in captivity. Historian Christopher Catherwood has called the siege 'the worst defeat of the Allies in World War I'.[4] Ten months later, the British Indian Army, consisting

---

[4]Catherwood, Christopher, *The Battles of World War I: Everything You Need*

almost entirely of newly recruited troops from western India, conquered Kut-al-Amara, Baghdad and other regions in the fall of Baghdad. In the campaign, 11,012 were killed, 3,985 died of wounds, 12,678 died of diseases, 13,492 were either missing or taken as prisoners (including the 8,000 prisoners from Kut-al-Amara) and an additional 51,836 were wounded.[5] For the British Empire, Mesopotamia was, in terms of casualties, cost and area, second only to the western front. By 1918, the Mesopotamian command was nearly half a million strong.[6] The Turkish 6th Army was finally defeated at the Battle of Sharqat, which took place between 23 and 30 October 1918. This was a week after the Armistice of Mudros was signed, which ended the war, and the state of Iraq became a British mandate. The Mesopotamian operations ended in November 1918, by which time the total casualties were over 63,000 soldiers.[7]

Names of many soldiers who sacrificed their lives in Kut-al-Amara are inscribed on the India Gate in New Delhi, built in 1931, under the Imperial War Graves Commission. This war memorial commemorates over 84,000 soldiers of the British Indian Army who lost their lives between 1914 and 1921 in the First World War, including in France, Flanders, Mesopotamia, Persia, East Africa and Gallipoli. The visiting Duke of Connaught laid the foundation stone on 10 February

---

to Know, Allison & Busby, United Kingdom, 2014.

[5]'Remembrance of Indian Army's Role in World War I', *Aviation and Defence Universe*, 11 November 2018, https://tinyurl.com/yvwwz5ah. Accessed on 7 August 2023.

[6]Latter, Edwin, 'The Indian Army in Mesopotamia 1914–1918, Part 2', *Journal of the Society for Army Historical Research*, Vol. 72, 1994, pp. 168–9, 172–3.

[7]'Siege and Surrender of Kut-el-Amara: Official Report of General Sir Percy Lake', 1916, *Current History (1916-1940)*, Vol. 5, No. 3, 1916, pp. 545–549.

1921. On the occasion, the Viceroy of India is reported to have said, 'The stirring tales of individual heroism, will live forever in the annals of this country' and that the memorial that was a tribute to the memory of the heroes 'known and unknown' would inspire future generations to endure hardships with similar fortitude and 'no less valour'. The Duke also read out a message from the King, which read, '"On this spot, in the central vista of the Capital of India, there will stand a Memorial Archway, designed to keep", in the thoughts of future generations, "the glorious sacrifice of the officers and men of the British Indian Army who fought and fell."'[8]

Ten years after the foundation stone laying ceremony, on 12 February 1931, the memorial was inaugurated by Lord Irwin, who on the occasion said, 'Those, who after us shall look upon this monument, may learn, in pondering its purpose something of that spirit of sacrifice and service, which the names upon its walls record.'[9]

As the war ended, on the international stage, India gained independent representation at the Paris Peace Conference in 1919. As a signatory of the Treaty of Versailles, it gained automatic entry into the League of Nations. Domestically, it paved the way for numerous organizational reforms in the army, the 'Indianization' of the army's officer corps and the formation of the Indian Air Force. It also set in motion the chain of events that eventually led to India's independence in August 1947.

---

[8]Arthur Duke of Connaught, *His Royal Highness the Duke of Connaught in India 1921: Being a Collection of the Speeches Delivered by His Royal Highness*, Superintendent Government Printing, Calcutta, 1921, pp. 68–72.
[9]Lord Irwin, Viceroy, *Speeches by Lord Irwin from 30th October 1929 to 18th April 1931*, Government of India Press, Simla, 1931, p. 328, https://tinyurl.com/3fayzmv5. Accessed on 7 August 2023.

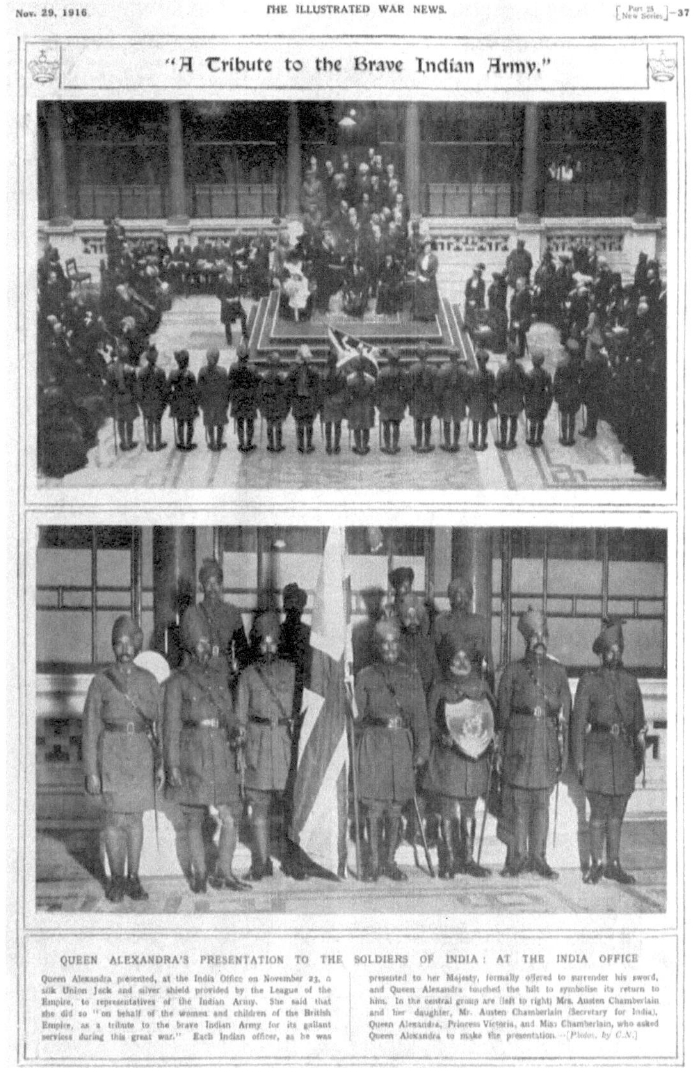

Nov. 29, 1916 THE ILLUSTRATED WAR NEWS. [Part 25 New Series]—37

"A Tribute to the Brave Indian Army."

QUEEN ALEXANDRA'S PRESENTATION TO THE SOLDIERS OF INDIA: AT THE INDIA OFFICE

Queen Alexandra presented, at the India Office on November 23, a silk Union Jack and silver shield provided by the League of the Empire, to representatives of the Indian Army. She said that she did so "on behalf of the women and children of the British Empire, as a tribute to the brave Indian Army for its gallant services during this great war." Each Indian officer, as he was presented to her Majesty, formally offered to surrender his sword, and Queen Alexandra touched the hilt to symbolise its return to him. In the central group are (left to right) Mrs. Austen Chamberlain and her daughter, Mr. Austen Chamberlain (Secretary for India), Queen Alexandra, Princess Victoria, and Miss Chamberlain, who asked Queen Alexandra to make the presentation.—[*Photos. by C.N.*]

Queen Alexandra's presentation to the soldiers of India at the India office

Source: The Illustrated War News – Volume 3

Among those present, both at the foundation laying ceremony and the inauguration ceremony of the India Gate, was Inder Mohan, who had survived the war against all odds. Having survived the war, it was time for Inder Mohan to take his next step. Indians had agreed to participate in the war as part of the British–Indian troops on the express assurance given by the British that Indians would be given a greater role in the administration of India after the war. But was this promise fulfilled?

3

Administrative Reforms in British India (1914–22)

The higher civil service in British India was formed under the Government of India Act, 1858, christened as the Imperial Civil Service, following the transfer of control and power from the East India Company to the British Crown. It was renamed as the Indian Civil Service (ICS) under the Indian Civil Services Act of 1861, and ruled over 300 million people of the country. The power of appointment was in the hands of the British, and indeed it was only the British who initially got appointed to the ICS. The mandatory exam was exclusively held in England.

The ICS was divided into separate departments: the executive, which administered the districts and collected the land revenues and taxes; the judicial, which provided judges for the district and high courts; the political, which provided officers for the diplomatic corps, and residents and agents in the princely states; and the secretariat, which provided senior officials for both the central and state governments. Below this came the largely Indian and uncovenanted civil servants of the police, medical and forestry services, and the agriculture and engineering departments.[1]

[1]Gonsalves, Trijita, 'From ICS to IAS: A Historical Review of the Civil Services in India', *ResearchGate*, September 2019, https://tinyurl.com/2z8bzhxv. Accessed on 24 July 2023.

The early part of the twentieth century saw an increased representation of Indians in the ICS. This was on account of two important factors. After the First World War, the interest among the British in joining the ICS declined. The pay scales were not lucrative enough, and many found better opportunities in Britain itself. The second factor was the increased political uncertainty in the country.

After his training in law, Gandhi's first job for an Indian company had required him to move to South Africa. The ruling white Boers (descendants of Dutch settlers) discriminated against all people of colour there. When railroad officials made Gandhi sit in a third-class coach even though he had purchased a first-class ticket, he refused, and the police forced him off the train. Such was the impact of this event on Gandhi that he decided to give up his lucrative law practice and dedicated himself to fight against all forms of oppression.

Gandhi became an outspoken critic of South Africa's discrimination policies. He vehemently and openly opposed the Boer legislature that enacted law requiring Indians to register with the police and be fingerprinted. Not only did he refuse to follow the mandate of this law but also motivated other Indians to follow his example. This may have been his first civil disobedience and non-co-operation movement, strategies he would emulate later in India. Gandhi was arrested and put in jail, the first of many times he would be imprisoned for disobeying what he saw as unjust laws.[2] The film *Gandhi* by Richard Attenborough shows Gandhi giving a speech to an audience, principally people of Indian origin.

---

[2]'Gandhi and Civil Disobedience', *Teach Democracy*, https://tinyurl.com/2xs7nk9p. Accessed on 7 December 2023.

He describes the laws introduced in South Africa:

> Let us begin by being clear about General Smuts' new law: All Indians must now be fingerprinted, like criminals, men, and women. No marriage, other than a Christian marriage, is considered valid. Under this Act, our wives and mothers are whores, and every man here is a bastard... And our policemen, passing an Indian dwelling—I will not call them homes—may enter and demand the card of any Indian woman whose dwelling it is.
>
> Understand, he does not have to stand at the door. He may enter.[3]

While in jail, Gandhi adopted the term 'civil disobedience' from the essay 'Civil Disobedience' by Henry David Thoreau, a nineteenth century American writer. It described his strategy of non-violently refusing to cooperate with injustice. Whilst heavily influenced by this form of protest, Gandhi preferred the Sanskrit word *satyagraha* (devotion to truth) for his civil disobedience movement, and following his release, he continued to protest the registration law by supporting labour strikes and organizing a massive non-violent march. Finally, the Boer government agreed to end the most objectionable parts of the registration law. Once again, Gandhi's policy of non-violence was captured effectively in the script of the film through his speech:

> I am asking you to fight! To fight against their anger, not to provoke it. We will not strike a blow, but we will receive them. And through our pain we will make them

---

[3]'Gandhi (1982)', *American Rhetoric: Movie Speech*, https://tinyurl.com/35f9mey5. Accessed on 1 November 2023.

> see their injustice, and it will hurt—as all fighting hurts. But we cannot lose. We cannot. They may torture my body, break my bones, even kill me. Then, they will have my dead body—not my obedience.[4]

After 20 years in South Africa, Gandhi, already famous in India owing to his successes in South Africa, came back to India in 1915, to a hero's welcome, with thousands greeting him as he got off the ship at the Apollo Bunder in Bombay (now Mumbai). Gandhi devoted the rest of his life to his struggle against what he considered three great evils afflicting India. The first of these was the British rule, which Gandhi believed impoverished the Indian people. The second evil was Hindu–Muslim disunity. And the third was the caste system prevalent in the country, discriminating against many christened as 'untouchables'. On the issue of British rule, Gandhi expected Britain to grant India greater independence after the First World War. When that did not happen, Gandhi called for strikes and other acts of peaceful civil disobedience. The British sometimes struck back with violence, but Gandhi insisted that Indians remain non-violent. Many answered Gandhi's call. But as the movement spread, Indians started rioting in some places. Gandhi called for order and cancelled protests. Though this step drew heavy criticism from fellow nationalists, Gandhi led a non-violent movement.

These and other such incidents made administering India increasingly difficult. As a result, the British aspirants for the ICS posts declined. There was also a rising pressure from the nationalist movement's proponents for increased Indian participation in the administration of the country.

---

[4]Ibid.

The ICS: A Coveted Career

In its efforts to recruit more ICS officers from India, in 1922, ICS examinations also started being held in India—first in Allahabad and then in Delhi. This was in keeping with the demand raised by the Indian National Congress (INC) in 1921. Prior to 1922, the examination could only be taken in England, and in 1868, the first Indian, Satyendranath Tagore, had gone to London to take the exam and also passed it. The Tatas, a prominent name in the Indian corporate sector, had set up a scholarship scheme to encourage more ICS officers from India, and as a result, by 1924, almost a third of the Indian ICS officers were Tata scholars.[5]

The ICS soon became the pinnacle of aspiration for educated Indians, and the social class from which the ICS was recruited also gave birth to many nationalist leaders. Jawaharlal Nehru once contemplated joining the ICS and Subhash Chandra Bose resigned soon after clearing the exam in 1921.[6] Later, on the basis of the recommendations of the Aitchison Committee, the minimum and maximum ages were increased from 19 and 21 years to 20 and 22, respectively. The candidates were allowed to take the examination both in London and India. A ratio of 50:50 was decided for the British and Indians as far as their intake in the ICS was concerned. In 1935, the British government decided to establish interim rule in the various provinces of India, which resulted in an exodus of the British subjects as civil servants, and as a result, the

---

[5]Kaushik, R.K., 'Indian Civil Service: Steel Frame of the British', *The Times of India, 23* April 2018, https://tinyurl.com/y8bacv85. Accessed 1 November 2023.

[6]Ibid.

number of Indian subjects in the ICS increased tremendously.

The recruits were men of impeccable honesty and known for their administrative capabilities. Though armed with extensive and absolute powers, they were the benevolent dictators, neither repressive nor authoritarian—attributes which the British Raj would become infamous for in the latter part of their rule. One reads about several examples of their benignity. Robin Gupta, a former civil servant,[7] narrated an example of how an illiterate old traveller on a train had thrown his railway ticket out of the window. In his mind, the transaction of buying the ticket and entering the train had been completed. When the ticket inspector tried to extort money, the hapless villager ran out of the train at the next station, straight to the house of the district magistrate, well past midnight, to seek his help.

Indeed, it was such administrative capabilities that gave India not only its rail network in the form of Indian Railways, but also several laws, like the Indian Penal Code, the Code of Criminal Procedure, the Indian Evidence Act and the Jail Manual. It was the British administration that developed the irrigation system, the Grand Trunk Road, the Indian Army and the defence services, an organized police force, and systematized educational and judicial systems. In fact, historians often rate the ICS as an important legacy of the British rule, placing it at par, if not on a higher pedestal, with the legal system, the Indian rail network and the Indian Army. David Lloyd George, the then PM of the UK, in a speech delivered on 2 August 1827, in the House of Commons on Indian Affairs, had said about the ICS: 'If you take the steel frame out of the fabric, it would collapse. There is one

---

[7]Gupta, Robin, 'The Raj and Its Civil Servants', *Rotary News*, September 2016, https://tinyurl.com/4bha4nk8. Accessed on 1 November 2023.

institution we will not cripple, there is one institution we will not deprive of its functions or of its privileges; and that is the institution which built up the British Raj—the British Civil Service in India.'

While the ICS was mainly in charge of administering India, it was an important arm of the British Raj with the mandate of securing and ensuring its dominance over the Indians. The ICS would thus be used in the later years for enforcing law and order during the civil disobedience movement, resulting in arrest and incarceration of many Indian leaders. Jawaharlal Nehru would state in one of his speeches how someone had once defined the ICS 'with which we are still afflicted in this country, as neither Indian, nor civil, nor a service'.[8]

Report, Revolt and Reform

Although reforms in the Indian administration by the British had begun before the war, the Indian participation in the war effort led Indians to expect concrete political gains vis-à-vis the British. These promises and the resultant expectations were not fully consummated, though they were also not altogether belied. On 20 August 1917, the Secretary of State, Lord Edwin Montagu, announced that the British Crown was now to be guided by the principle of 'the increasing association of Indians in every branch of the administration and the gradual development of self-governing institutions with a view to the progressive realisation of responsible government in India as an integral part of the British Empire'.[9]

---

[8]Nehru, Jawaharlal, *Glimpses of World History: Being Further Letters to His Daughter*, Lindsay Drummond Ltd, 1949.

[9]Burra, Arudra, 'The Indian Civil Service and the Raj: 1919–1950', *SSRN*, 7 May 2012, https://tinyurl.com/8bs8m2y2. Accessed on 1 November 2023.

The Anarchical and Revolutionary Crimes Act of 1919, popularly (or unpopularly) known as the Rowlatt Act, was passed on the recommendations of the Rowlatt Committee and named after its president, Sir Sidney Rowlatt. The report on Indian constitutional reforms by the Secretary of State for India, Edwin Montagu, and the Viceroy, Lord Chelmsford (also called the 'Montagu–Chelmsford Report') was published eight months later, and it laid the basis for the Government of India Act, 1919, which came into force in 1921. The main recommendation of the report was that control over some aspects of provincial government be passed to Indian ministers responsible to an Indian electorate.

Indians did not greet the Montagu–Chelmsford Reforms with elation. Many Indians, like Inder Mohan, had fought alongside the British in the First World War and thus expected much greater concessions. In fact, the Congress and the Muslim League had come together demanding self-rule, as the 1919 reforms did not satisfy the political demands of Indians. Despite the losses suffered by Britain during the war, any opposition to the British rule was repressed by imposition of restrictions on the press and on movement by re-enacting the anarchical reforms. Any person suspected of terrorism was to be imprisoned for up to two years without a trial. It gave the colonial authorities power to deal with all revolutionary activities. This unpopular legislation provided for stricter control of the press, arrests without warrant, indefinite detention without trial and juryless in-camera trials for proscribed political acts. The accused were denied the right to know the accusers and the evidence used in the trial.[10]

---

[10]Vohra, Ranbir, *Making of India: A Historical Survey*, M.E. Sharpe, 2001.

These measures were pushed through the Imperial Legislative Council despite the unanimous opposition of its Indian members. Several members of the council, including Muhammad Ali Jinnah, resigned in protest. Indians saw this as a betrayal of their strong support for the British war effort.

On 6 April 1919, Gandhi launched a nationwide protest against the Rowlatt Act, with the peak of the protest seen in the state of Punjab. The situation worsened in Amritsar as the protests intensified. The Punjab government met the protesters with great repression, which eventually led to the infamous Jallianwala Bagh massacre. On 13 April, General Reginald Dyer ordered his troops to block the entrance to the park and opened fire at the gathered crowds. The troops fired non-stop for almost 10 minutes, aiming their guns at hapless Indians running to save their lives, till their ammunition ran out. Over 1,650 rounds were fired resulting in the deaths of 379 civilians and injuring 1,200. Among the dead and injured were unarmed men, women and children who had gathered for a peaceful protest and to celebrate the festival of Baisakhi.

The Hunter Commission, which examined Dyer post the incident, narrated Dyer's own damning testimony where he admitted that he knew that he could have dispersed the crowds without firing but chose not to do so because 'they would have come back again and laughed'.[11] Dyer had also attempted to take with him a machine gun mounted on an armoured vehicle, which was too large to be taken through the narrow entrance gate of the park. When asked by the Hunter Commission whether he would have used the

[11]Saha, Abhishek, 'I Had to Fire Well: Jallianwala Bagh Butcher Gen Dyer's Testimony', *Hindustan Times*, 15 April 2015, https://tinyurl.com/3d3jy52c. Accessed on 1 November 2023.

machine gun to kill even more, Dyer unhesitatingly answered in the affirmative. Even though there were many women and children amongst the wounded, he said he saw no reason why they should be assisted in the aftermath.[12]

Kishwar Desai in her book titled *Jallianwala Bagh, 1919: The Real Story* reproduced some portions from the Hunter Commission inquiry. She writes:

> Justice Rankin, cross-examined General Dyer about his shooting an unarmed crowd at Jallianwala Bagh: You thought it necessary to take action on the analogy of a state of war?
>
> Dyer: Quite so, I looked upon these people who had rebelled as enemies of the Crown.
>
> Sir C. L. Setalvad, Cross-examining Dyer: Did it occur to you that you were really doing great disservice by driving discontent?
>
> Dyer: No. I thought it was my duty to do it…and any man, any reasonable being with a sense of justice, would see that I was doing a merciful act, and that they ought to be thankful to me for doing it.[13]

Lala Lajpat Rai, commenting on the massacre, wrote:

> Benevolent Imperialism is like a caged lion. However, you may play with it so long as it is caged or under the spell of a master-tamer; the moment it gets out of control it is bound to behave in conformity with its

[12]Habib, Irfan, 'Jallianwala Bagh Massacre: The First Wave of Mass Struggle and Its Aftermath, 1919–26', *Social Scientist*, Vol. 47, No. 5/6, 2019, pp. 3–8.

[13]Desai, Kishwar, *Jallianwala Bagh, 1919: The Real Story*, Westland Limited, 2019.

> real nature. The atrocities perpetuated at Amritsar have proved that Imperialism run mad is more dangerous, more vindictive, more inhuman, than a frenzied uncontrollable mob.[14]

Dyer's efforts were lauded by many sections of the British society, including members of the House of Lords. While praising Dyer without hesitation, they put the entire blame of the incident on Gandhi: 'Mr Gandhi, posing as a Mahatma and arrogating to himself a religious sanctity to which he has no claim, introduced his Satyagraha or passive resistance, which quickly developed into active defiance of the law, accompanied by the wildest excesses.'[15]

Despite the laudations, the Hunter Commission recommended that General Dyer be dismissed. But, as he was considered a soldier acting on orders, he could not be tried for having committed mass murder.

The Jallianwala Bagh massacre was a turning point when it came to Indo-British political relations. There were many 'moderate' Indian politicians, such as Motilal Nehru, who were radicalized. In fact, a few, like Sir Sankaran Nair resigned in protest from the Imperial Legislative Council, and then there was Rabindranath Tagore, the famous Indian poet, who returned his knighthood. Gandhi regretted the Rowlatt agitation as a 'Himalayan blunder' because it was taken up by people who were yet untrained in the philosophy and practice

---

[14]Bakaya, Ravi M., and Pandit Pearay Mohan, *The Punjab 'Rebellion' of 1919 and How It Was Suppressed: An Account of the Punjab Disorders and the Working of Martial Law*, Gyan Publishing House, 1999.

[15]Doctor, Vikram, 'General Dyer: The Man Behind the Jallianwala Bagh Massacre', *The Economic Times*, 14 April 2019, https://tinyurl.com/sahdm79z. Accessed on 24 July 2023.

of non-violent agitation. Following that, the protest was soon called off.[16]

In December 1920, Gandhi moved a resolution in favour of non-cooperation for *purna swaraj* (complete self-rule) and urged the boycott of foreign goods, which included, in particular, British cloth, the relinquishment of titles, the withdrawal from law courts, government schools and colleges and the legislative councils. It provided for civil disobedience in case its political demands were not met. Interestingly, Gandhi explicitly clarified that the call for non-cooperation did not extend to a plea for government servants to leave their jobs. Nevertheless, the call for non-cooperation put Indians in the ICS—many of them from the same social stratum as those in the nationalist movement—in an awkward and ambivalent position. Even though Indians in the ICS were not called on to resign, the general thrust of the movement was, after all, clearly towards a disengagement from British institutions.[17]

According to the author Arudra Burra who interviewed many ICS officers for his book, *The Indian Civil Service and the Raj: 1919–1950*, some Indian candidates nominated to the ICS in 1919 'expressed their misgivings at their particularly unenviable position between the upper and nether millstones of a provincial government and the non-co-operators'. According to author Phillip Woodruff, the ICS complained about the 'bitter political feeling', the 'racial hatred' and the 'poison gas' released by the non-cooperation movement.[18]

---

[16]Burra, Arudra, 'The Indian Civil Service and the Raj: 1919–1950', *SSRN*, 7 May 2012, https://tinyurl.com/8bs8m2y2. Accessed on 1 November 2023.

[17]Ibid.

[18]Woodruff, Philip, *The Men Who Ruled India: The Founders*, J. Cape, United Kingdom, 1953.

I.M. Lall Joins ICS

These facts set the backdrop against which Inder Mohan was going to join the ICS. Owing to the political unrest and uncertainty and the demand of the Indian nationalists for an increased share in administration, the recruitment of Indian ICS officers increased steadily from 1919. Indians did make it to the ICS as early as in 1864, but their numbers were low. By 1892, 30 years after the exams were first conducted, only 25 Indians had joined the ICS. In 1915, the figure had risen to 63, comprising 5 per cent of the total strength. This proportion rose dramatically in the 1920s and 1930s.[19]

D.D. Saigal, my maternal grandfather, was an officer in the Indian Forest Service (IFS). He authored a book titled, *Footprints on Sand*, in which he chronicled:

> The exploits of the Indian Army in all theatres of the war were specially noted, but the main aim of the student community remained the civil service or the other learned professions like law, medicine etc. It was around this time that an attempt was made to raise a student's corps and a Punjab University Signal Corps (also known as Double Company). This corps saw service in Mesopotamia, now a part of Iraq, and its exploits were eulogised by the Army authorities. At one time the whole corps was in fear of annihilation but was saved by the gallantry of its sergeant who later proved to be an able administrator as a member of the Indian Civil Service. On demobilisation, all members of the corps were offered lucrative appointments.[20]

---

[19]Ibid.

[20]Saigal, D.D. *Footprints on Sand: An Autobiography*, Yash Publications, India, 2014.

In late 1918, after the First World War, Inder Mohan would have been roughly 21–22 years old. The upper limit of eligibility for the ICS was initially 21, which was then increased to 22. According to some records, for those recruited in the ICS from the army, the age limit did not apply. By 1920, there were five methods of entry into the higher civil service: first, the open competitive examinations held in London; second, separate competitive examinations in India; third, nomination in India to satisfy provincial and communal representation; fourth, promotion from the Provincial Civil Service; and finally, appointments from the bar. One-fourth of the posts in the ICS were filled from the bar.

I.M. Lall
Source: Lall family albums

When Inder Mohan returned from Mesopotamia, he applied to join the ICS and was called to London to appear for an interview. He hailed from a not-so-affluent family and didn't have the wherewithal to afford a trip to London. He had a rich maternal uncle from whom he borrowed money to make the trip. He reached London, appeared for the interview and passed. He would return to India having achieved his dream of being appointed as an ICS officer.

Having completed his law degree, Inder Mohan was recruited on the judicial side of the ICS. He also took the ICS exam in London and joined the ICS on 2 October 1922.

He was allowed to count one year for pension in regard of his war services. He served various districts as assistant commissioner until 1928, when he was appointed sessions judge of Sheikhupura.

4

Family Affairs (1923-39)

Back at home, Dropadi and her family were very apprehensive about Inder Mohan's return to Mianwali. After all, he was now a well-educated man and an ICS officer. A girl from a small village of Mianwali may not be his preferred choice of life partner. However, Inder Mohan's mother, who was referred to as Amma, was confident that her son would return. She would assure Dropadi's family that not only would he return but also marry her.

Inder Mohan did fulfil his promise and returned to Mianwali, where he married Daulat Bai Chawla in 1923. Her name was changed to Dropadi thereafter. They had nine children. Their first child, Narayan Dutt, was born sometime in 1924. He died almost immediately after birth, suffering from diphtheria. The date of his death is unknown. Tilak Raj was the second child, born on 21 March 1925 in Mianwali. The third child, Amar Raj, was born in Amritsar on 15 March 1928. The next was the first daughter, Savitri, born on 6 August 1929 in Ludhiana, Punjab. Sheila was born on 8 October 1930 in Mianwali. Chander was born on 5 April 1932. It is unclear whether Chander was born in Mianwali or Peshawar. The next child was Mool Raj (Billy), born in March 1934. Pushpa followed next; her birthday is unknown. She died young, in 1947. The last was Jag Mohan (Jogi) born on 1 January 1939 in Peshawar, North-West Frontier Province (NWFP).

Life in the ICS

Inder Mohan resided in several different cities, including Lahore and Ambala. He served as sessions judge from 1929 and was made permanent in July 1934.

Life as children of an ICS officer was nothing less than royalty. The ICS consisted largely of Englishmen coming over from England to rule the country. Hence, the lifestyle of the Indian ICS officers was also royal, and they too developed, so to say, English habits. Inder Mohan hosted elaborate parties, no different from those hosted by the colonial rulers, where all the children dressed up. The house had the normal ICS standard staff consisting of seven to eight servants, a chef, an assistant chef and two bearers. This staff would regularly help in hosting parties for 15 to 20 guests, or more, for a formal sit-down dinner. Owing to a shortage of other sources of entertainment at the time, the only leisure activities in a small town were either a visit to the club where one could play bridge or sports, like tennis and billiards, or attending house parties. Visits to each other' homes for parties were also a norm, with the attendees being more or less the same. After all, there were only a few people who were in the position of attending those gatherings. The parties were always elaborate, with Dropadi as the hostess taking well over two days to complete the preparations, and then another two days thereafter to wind up. This involved removal of the silverware and crockery, giving them a thorough cleaning before use, and tidying things up after the party. Good old Brasso and Silvo were the preferred cleaners. It was nothing less than mini royalty.

As the ICS was the highest service, called the heaven-born or the steel frame of the British, it offered high salaries and perks along with power for decision-making. The monthly salary of a district collector was ₹1,100; commissioner, ₹3,000; a High Court judge, ₹4,000; a High Court Chief Justice, ₹5,000; and that of a financial commissioner, ₹3,500. The governor's salary was ₹8,333+£300 (₹450).[1] For perspective, in 1940, gold sold at ₹14 a gram, while in 2023, it is above ₹6,000. Hence, a rupee in 1940 would be approximately ₹428 in 2023, taking the lowest salary, that of the district collector, to a current equivalent of ₹376,200. Add to this, the palatial house and other perks. By any standard, these were princely sums.

To explain the scale of the homes that they lived in, Amar often narrated the story of the carpet that found a place of pride in our home in Panchsheel Park, New Delhi. Significant portion of the carpet were destroyed by carpet bugs and had to be cut away. The carpet was so big that despite the removal of a large part, it could still not fit in the spacious drawing room in our house. This carpet, in all its glory and at its full size, used to fit in the middle of the drawing room of Inder Mohan's house in Ambala, with sufficient space left on all four sides. The carpet, in my estimation, would have been over 15 ft by 15 ft in its original state.

Trouble in Paradise (1935–37)

The eventful year that forms the core of this book was 1935. While Inder Mohan was performing his duties as the district and sessions court judge in Multan, he learnt that the staff

---

[1]Kaushik, R.K., 'Tracing the History of Civil Services Recruitment', *The Tribune*, 13 May 2008, https://tinyurl.com/2rf6b63w. Accessed on 27 July 2023.

under him, acting under the stewardship of the clerk of court, were indulging in nefarious activities. They would reach out to litigants whose cases were pending before Inder Mohan and offer to get a decision in their favour. They would take hefty sums of money from the litigants under the garb of extending it to Inder Mohan as his bribe. To camouflage their opprobrious conduct, they offered a money-back guarantee. If the decision went against the person, the money would promptly be returned on the pretext that Judge sahib had decided to return the money citing that the case was such a difficult one that he could not, under any circumstance, decide in their favour. When Inder Mohan learnt of this, he was aghast and immediately initiated disciplinary action against them. This disciplinary action caused a stir amongst the employees working under him, and this stir would manifest in unpleasant ways in the near future.

Contemporaneously, in early 1935, Inder Mohan, whilst stationed in Hoshiarpur, enlisted Sunder Das, a nephew of his wife, as subordinate staff in one of the courts under his control. In May 1935, as Inder Mohan was transferred to Multan, Sunder Das also petitioned to be transferred to Multan. Responding to the same, Inder Mohan appointed Sunder Das as *ahlmad* (a court employee) in August 1936 to one of the sub-judges under him, in an officiating arrangement.

The appointment of Sunder Das and the action taken against his other subordinates created its own tribulations. In April 1936, Inder Mohan went on a leave to England. One of the employees against whom action had been initiated influenced the incumbent, who had taken charge in Multan in his absence, to remove Sunder Das from his post. The idea was to ultimately put pressure on Inder Mohan to withdraw the disciplinary action taken against the other employees.

On 22 October 1936, Inder Mohan resumed charge as district and sessions judge, Multan. When he heard about the removal of Sunder Das and the reasons for his removal, he forthwith signed a proposal for Sunder Das to be appointed ahlmad at the sub-judge's court in Leiah (now Layyah). On 23 December 1936, Inder Mohan passed an administrative order for the confirmation of Sunder Das in place of an official who had retired. This order would have had the effect of promoting Sunder Das over the heads of a number of subordinate officials senior to him. This act further brought more employees in acrimony against Inder Mohan, and they took steps to file a petition against the order.

Within three months of Sunder Das taking charge, aided and abetted by the recalcitrant employees, the clerk of court put up a note before Inder Mohan explaining that a mistake had been made and that the vacancy in which Sunder Das had been appointed actually did not exist and suggested the cancellation of his last order of appointment of Sunder Das. Inder Mohan was not going to bend under pressure. He proceeded to pass a series of orders, which included confirmation of Sunder Das as a paid candidate.

In the course of these actions, Inder Mohan was transferred to the NWFP and took charge as district and sessions judge on 15 April 1937. Before his transfer, Inder Mohan also passed a number of orders affecting some of the junior officials who had protested against the order of 23 December 1936 of appointment of Sunder Das. In an order of 4 March 1937, he directed the posting of one of them to Alipore, considered to be a particularly unpleasant station. By one of the orders made on 22 March 1937, he confirmed a proposal by the clerk of court to transfer two others from headquarters in Multan to Muzaffargarh and Khanewal as a disciplinary action. By another order, he reduced their seniority, and before he left Multan, he recorded adverse remarks in the service books of four of the persons who had protested.

A cocktail of trouble was brewing, and the cherry on top was his posting at the NWFP.

∞

5

I.M. Lall in the North-West Frontier Province (1935–38)

The posting in the NWFP was of special interest to Inder Mohan. The township of Takht-i-Bahi in the Gandhara[1] region of what is now Pakistan, which boasts some of the most important ancient monasteries of Buddhism, were under his jurisdiction. Takht-i-Bahi, literally translated as 'throne of origins', contained a monastic complex founded in the early first century. The monastery was in continuous use till the seventh century AD.

Inder Mohan was a collector and an archaeologist by hobby. During his tenure in the NWFP, he undertook extensive travels in the region, which included trips to Takht-i-Bahi. Owing to the location of the monastery on the high hills, it had escaped invasions and was reasonably well preserved. However, its ongoing preservation under the British was somewhat lax.

---

[1]Gandhara was an ancient region in the Peshawar basin in the northwest of the ancient Indian subcontinent, corresponding to present-day northwest Pakistan and northeast Afghanistan. The centre of the region was at the confluence of Kabul and Swat rivers, bounded by the Sulaiman Mountains on the west and the Indus on the east.

Buddha statues from Takht-i-Bahi
Source: Lall family albums

The Roerich Pact

Contemporaneous to Inder Mohan's posting in Multan and thereafter in Peshawar, on 15 April 1935, the Treaty on the Protection of Artistic and Scientific Institutions and Historic Monuments was concluded and signed by representatives of 21 American states at the White House. This pact was the conclusion of an initiative by a well-known and renowned painter, writer, archaeologist, theosophist and public figure,

Nicholas Roerich. The pact came to be known as the 'Roerich Pact'. Rabindranath Tagore, writing to Nicholas Roerich, said:

> I have keenly followed your most remarkable achievements in the realm of Arts and also your great humanitarian work for the welfare of the nations, of which your Peace Pact ideal with a special Banner for the protection of cultural treasures is a singularly effective symbol. I feel sure that it will have far-reaching effects on the cultural harmony of nations.[2]

Born in Russia, Roerich, along with his wife Helena and two sons George and Svetoslav, had left Russia and emigrated to Finland after the October revolution and the acquisition of power by Vladimir Lenin's Bolshevik party. Later, Roerich had relocated to London with his family in mid-1919, and in the autumn of 1920, they had travelled to America, where the family stayed till 1923.

Being deeply interested in theosophical mysticism, the obvious choice of country for Roerich was India. In London, he had befriended the famed British Buddhist, Christmas Humphreys, the philosopher–author H.G. Wells, and the poet and Nobel laureate Rabindranath Tagore.

In 1923, Roerich, the 'practical idealist', set out to the Himalayas with Helena and George. Roerich had initially settled in Darjeeling in the same house that the thirteenth Dalai Lama had stayed in during his exile in India. He had briefly gone back to America only to return and join George and six of his friends on the five-year Roerich Asian Expedition,

---

[2]Singh, Kavita, '"Mountain Muse"–An Exploration to Human Consciousness and Eternity', *Gyankosh: An Interdisciplinary E-Journal*, Vol. I, 2018, https://tinyurl.com/3uzx97zd. Accessed on 1 November 2023.

which started from Sikkim through Punjab, Kashmir, Ladakh, the Karakoram Mountains, Khotan, Kashgar, Qara Shar, Urumchi, Irtysh, the Altai Mountains, the outer region of Mongolia, the Central Gobi, Kansu, Tsaidam and Tibet with a detour through Siberia to Moscow. The official mission of his expedition, as Roerich put it, was to act as the ambassador of Western Buddhism to Tibet. To the Western media, it was presented as an artistic and scientific enterprise.

This expedition was finally and forcibly stopped in Tibet, where he had been detained and forced to live in tents in sub-zero conditions and subsist on meagre rations. Five men of the expedition had died during this time. In March 1928, the survivors were allowed to leave Tibet, and they trekked south to settle in India, where they founded a research centre, the Himalayan Forest Research Institute. Roerich's son Svetsolav later married the renowned Indian actress and the first lady of Indian cinema, Devika Rani, who incidentally was also the grand-niece of Rabindranath Tagore.[3]

The paths of Roerich and Inder Mohan crossed in Takht-i-Bahi over the preservation of the ruins of the monastic complex and the Gandhara statutes. Whilst Inder Mohan and Roerich were aligned in maintaining the statues, sculptures and figurines in India itself, the British Raj had other ideas. This led to obvious tensions between the Raj and Inder Mohan. After all, Inder Mohan was still considered as a subject of the Empire and a person whose position as an ICS officer was dependent upon the pleasure of His Majesty. His job was to support the Crown and its policies and not to challenge them.

---

[3]Andreyev, Alexandre, *Soviet Russia and Tibet: The Debacle of Secret Diplomacy, 1918-1930s*, Brill, Boston, 2003.

Buddha statues from Takht-i-Bahi
Source: Lall family albums

Inder Mohan wholeheartedly supported Roerich's appeal to protect cultural property and maintain them as Indian heritage. The British, on the other hand, felt that whatever was in India was their personal property. Roerich also had support from other Indian luminaries like Jagdish Bose, S. Radhakrishnan, C.V. Raman, James Cousins, and many others.

Indian organizations, such as the Allahabad Municipal Museum, Bharat Kala Bhawan in Banaras, the Maha Bodhi Society, the Indian Women Association and almost the entire mass media expressed their commitment to the Roerich Pact. However, it was owing to the opposition by the British that it could be accepted by India only after its independence. In 1948, under the leadership of Jawaharlal Nehru, India approved the Roerich Pact and raised the Banner of Peace. Indeed, despite best efforts, one can still find many statues from Takht-i-Bahi on display in the British Museum in London.

The Empire Strikes (1937)

wife's relative, Sundar Das, without regard to rules or the rights of others.

(2) Victimization of those whose rights had been infringed and who tried to assert them.

As regards (1) the facts are :-

(a) Mr. Lal gave his wife's nephew, Sundar Das, a resident of Mianwali, employment as Ahlmad in Kangra, when he was District Judge, Hoshiarpur (charge 1).

(b) When he himself was appointed District Judge, Multan, he arranged for Sundar Das's transfer to Muzaffargarh and appointed him as Ahlmad at Leiah, the nearest place in the Multan Division to Sundar Das's home in Mianwali (charge 2).

(c) When Mr. Lal went on leave in 1936, Sundar Das was reverted by Mr. Bedi, who succeeded Mr. Lal as Sessions Judge, but on his return from leave Mr. Lal reposted Sundar Das, and (charge 3) confirmed him on 23rd December 1936 over the heads of several people senior to him.

(d) When the order of confirmation became known, there was an outcry and many appeals and representations. Mr. Lal then cancelled his order confirming Sundar Das, on the ground that there really was in fact no vacancy in which he could be confirmed, but the same day (charge 5) he appointed Sundar Das as a paid candidate over the heads of others and continued him at Leiah.

Charges 1 and 2 are admitted by Mr. Lal. As regards charge 2, he states that he was unaware of the rules, which should have precluded the transfer of Sundar Das from Kangra to Muzaffargarh; but the gravamen of the charge against him is not the breach of rules, but Mr. Lal's improper and unseemly conduct in taking his wife's relative about with him.

As regards charges 3 and 5, he blames his Clerk of Court, Chaman Lal, for misleading him and pleads that he put matters right by cancelling his order of December 23rd confirmin[g]

Charges of nepotism against I.M. Lall
Source: National Archives of India

The Empire did not take kindly to Inder Mohan's open support for Roerich. Its ire would, however, manifest itself in the most devious and duplicitous manner. The topic of Indian heritage and its protection was a sensitive one. By now the

Indian nationalist movement under Gandhi was reaching a crescendo. The Crown would have to deploy some means to remove Inder Mohan. He had become a thorn in the Empire's side, and his removal had become necessary.

The disgruntled employees against whom Inder Mohan had initiated disciplinary action became an obvious ally of the Crown. They congregated to set up a case to remove Inder Mohan from service.

In September 1937, whilst Inder Mohan was serving in Peshawar in the NWFP, he received a letter (D.O. letter No C.S.1, dated 2 September 1937) from the judicial commissioner, enclosing a letter from the chief secretary to NWFP government, informing the judicial commissioner that the Punjab government had decided to hold a departmental enquiry into the conduct of Inder Mohan under Rule 55, Civil Services (Classification, Control and Appeal) Rules[4]. Significantly, the inquiry was related to the period when Inder Mohan was stationed in Multan. The letter contained eight charges against him, of which copies were enclosed. The charges were listed as follows:[5]

(a) Mr Lall gave his wife's nephew, Sunder Das, a resident of Mianwali, employment as ahlmad in Kangra, when he was district judge, Hoshiarpur (charge 1).

(b) When he himself was appointed district judge, Multan, he arranged for Sunder Das's transfer to Muzaffargarh and appointed him as ahlmad at Leiah, the nearest place in the Multan Division to Sunder Das's home in Mianwali (charge 2).

(c) When Mr Lall went on a leave in 1936, Sunder Das

[4]Now the Central Civil Services (Classification, Control and Appeal) Rules

[5]As reproduced in the High Court decision titled 'I.M. Lall v Secretary of State (AIR 1944 Lahore 240)', a copy of which is in the possession of the author

was removed by Mr Bedi, who succeeded Mr Lall as sessions judge. But on his return from leave, Mr Lall reposted Sunder Das, and (charge 3) confirmed him on 23 December 1936 over the needs of several people senior to him.[6]

(d) When the order of confirmation became known, there was an outcry and many appeals and representations. Mr Lall then cancelled his order confirming Sunder Das, on the ground that there really was in fact no vacancy in which he could be confirmed, but the same day (charge 5), he appointed Sunder Das as paid candidate over the heads of others and continued him at Leiah.

As regards the charges of victimization, the facts were listed as follows:

> Five clerks presented petitions against Mr Lall's order of 23 December about confirming Sunder Das. Before leaving the district at the end of March 1937, he cancelled the same but gave him another petty job,

(a) Wrote adverse reports in the Service Books of four of them (charge 8),
(b) Transferred two of them to the worst out-stations in the division, (charge 6) and
(c) Inflicted excessive punishment on one of them for a trivial offence (charge 7).[7]

---

[6]The fourth charge was related to the alleged delay in communicating certain orders to the office.

[7]As reproduced in the High Court decision titled 'I.M. Lall v Secretary of State (AIR 1944 Lahore 240)'

Inder Mohan was called upon to furnish a written statement in his defence. At the end of each charge, the witnesses—or documents whereby it was proposed to prove the charge—were indicated.

Near the end of the letter were two paragraphs interposed, which clearly revealed more than they hid, containing a clear threat to Inder Mohan. It read:

> That the above facts and his failure to offer any sufficient explanation up to the present are sufficient to prove that he had abused his position as an officer entrusted with power of appointment on behalf of the Crown to show favour to a relation of his to the detriment of other officials serving under him, in contravention both of the recognised principles governing the conduct of Government servants as well as of the express orders of Government, and that he further abused his position as an officer entrusted with powers of discipline over other officers of the Crown to persecute various persons who sought to protect their own interests in a legitimate manner. That he should show cause why he should not be dismissed, removed, or reduced or subjected to such other disciplinary action as the competent authority may think fit to enforce for breach of Government rules and conduct unbecoming to a member of the Indian Civil Service.[8]

It is significant to note here that at no point prior to the receipt of this letter had he been consulted or an explanation sought for his actions. His superiors had simply proceeded to issue this letter, which in its tone and tenor already held him

---

[8]As reproduced in the High Court decision titled 'I.M. Lall v Secretary of State (AIR 1944 Lahore 240)', a copy of which is in the possession of the author

guilty of the charges. The writing on the wall was quite clear: the Empire had decided to terminate the services of Inder Mohan. Many years later, in his petition to the Privy Council, Inder Mohan wrote:

> In my case from the very beginning it was intended to dismiss or remove me from the ICS. In this connection I would request Your Majesty to send for the minutes of the proceedings of a meeting of the Hon'ble Judges of the Lahore High Court. The Honourable Chief Justice is reported to have said at the meeting that I should be dismissed from service. Other Judges opposed this proposal and it was decided to report the matter to the Government.[9]

Inder Mohan realized that hereon, maintaining a paper trail would be important. He had been a judge long enough to know where the inquiry was headed. Whilst preparing his detailed written response, not only did he ask for complete documents which were to be used against him but also took the position that there was no necessity of an oral inquiry in this matter, as all his orders were in writing. According to him, even the materials sought to be used against him were in writing and, on the basis of these materials, the government could give their decision.

Anderson's Inquiry and Consequences

Shortly thereafter, J.D. Anderson, ICS and commissioner, Rawalpindi division, was appointed to hold the departmental inquiry on 10 June 1938. Anderson was a celebrated officer

[9]Author possesses a copy of the said document in his personal archives.

accorded the title of Companion of the Indian Empire, an order of chivalry founded by Queen Victoria on 1 January 1878.

Anderson examined Inder Mohan on the raised charges. Inder Mohan dealt with each charge at considerable length, and this examination was produced in writing on 11 June 1938. Having recorded Inder Mohan's statement, Anderson considered it necessary to record a statement by Lala Chaman Lall, the clerk of court in Inder Mohan's sessions court in Multan. This examination took place in the presence of Inder Mohan, who was also permitted to ask whatever questions he desired. His statement was recorded on 30 July 1938. During the examination, difficult questions were put to the clerk by Inder Mohan, in the presence of Anderson. From his very demeanour and evasive responses, it became quite apparent that the clerk did not have good answers against the charges of corruption raised by Inder Mohan. Anderson's conclusion at the end of this examination was that the clerk was clearly not revealing the complete truth. Inder Mohan's version of the events seemed more plausible to him. Interestingly, Chaman Lall was later suspended by the Chief Justice on charges of corruption in judicial cases, a charge which Inder Mohan had also made against him.

After the examination, Anderson neither considered it necessary to examine any other witnesses nor did Inder Mohan apply for leave to examine any other witnesses. Based on his inquest, on 9 August 1938, Anderson presented his report, which read that Inder Mohan pleaded guilty to the first two charges dealing with the enlistment and transfer of Sunder Das to Multan and to the signing of the order of 23 December 1936. The remaining charges, Anderson found, on the basis of the evidence before him, were unproven. This is how he recorded his finding in Para 2 on the seventh page of his report: 'On the evidence, charge No 5 is not established against Mr Lall. It follows automatically that charge No 6 also fails and when these two charges are unproven, charges 7 and 8 cannot be established.'

In the next paragraph on the same page, he summed up his findings in these words, 'On the evidence before me I hold that charges 4–8 unproven.' Anderson's report went on to suggest possible options as an outcome of the inquiry: (1) orders should be passed on those charges only to which Inder Mohan had pleaded guilty, leaving the question of his guilt on the other charges undecided; or (2) to hold that, as the clerk of court was clearly not revealing the complete truth, Inder Mohan's word should be accepted and the last six charges should be taken as broken down for lack of proof; or (3) that anything Anderson had done should be regarded as a preliminary inquiry only and that some other officer should be appointed to make a complete investigation. Anderson proceeded to express his view that the third option was the proper course. In the concluding paragraphs of his report, he indicated that if he was required to give a final report, he would wish to look into further documents and matters before coming to final conclusions.[10]

The Crown clearly was not satisfied with Anderson's report. Their frustration could be gauged by the occurrences that succeeded it. Inder Mohan was immediately directed to return to Punjab and was posted in Lyallpur, where he joined on 10 November 1937. Vide a letter dated 18 October 1937, he was given a week to pack and depart, which was extended by five days at his request. Inder Mohan in his appeal to the Privy Council recorded how this 'transfer was unexpected and was ordered to humiliate and harass him'.[11]

[10]Author possesses a copy of the said document in his personal archives.

[11]Ibid.

Adding to this indignity, Inder Mohan, a confirmed district and sessions judge, was asked to join at a lower level, as an additional district and sessions judge in Lyallpur. An officer from the ICS, he was made to report to a junior officer from the Provincial Civil Service. He submitted ruefully, 'I do not know what idea the Government had in placing me under such a junior officer, but the job to which I was posted was also of a junior officer and I relieved a junior P.C.S officer.'[12]

As if with a predetermined disposition, the Crown decided to accept the third suggestion in the Anderson Report and appointed F.L. Brayne, also an ICS officer and CIE, and at the time, commissioner rural reconstruction, Punjab. His mandate was to complete Anderson's preliminary inquiry.

Brayne was a decorated British officer who had passed the competitive examination for appointment to the ICS in 1905. Most importantly, his loyalties to the Crown were beyond doubt. He was sent to Punjab, where he worked for some time as secretary to Delhi municipality during the period when the planning for New Delhi was underway. During the First World War, he served with the 18th Lancers of the British Indian Army, being mostly based in the Middle East. He was appointed as temporary lieutenant in June 1915, and the Kingdom of Serbia awarded him the Order of St Sava, fifth class, in 1917. He was awarded the Military Cross in 1919 while serving as a temporary lieutenant in Egypt 'for conspicuous gallantry and initiative'. After the war, Brayne returned to Punjab and became district officer of Gurgaon, at a time when the area had a population of around 700,000.[13]

---

[12]Ibid.

[13]Dewey, Clive, *Anglo-Indian Attitudes: Mind of the Indian Civil Service*, Bloomsbury, United Kingdom, 1993.

6

A Rushed Second Inquiry

While Inder Mohan was trying to build up his defence against the attempts to remove him from service, at the national level, the independence movement was gaining momentum. Many of the foremost nationalist politicians—Mahatma Gandhi, Motilal Nehru, Jawaharlal Nehru, Muhammad Ali Jinnah, Sardar Vallabhbhai Patel, Sir Tej Bahadur Sapru, B.R. Ambedkar to name a few—were lawyers. This led the British to disparage the legal profession for, amongst other things, being a class of 'trouble-makers'.[1] Inder Mohan was an officer who largely carried out his duties in an apolitical fashion and did not pander to the whims of the British rulers. Perhaps, he too was categorized by the British to be a troublemaker, and they did not want to put this inquiry to rest by accepting one of the possible conclusions recommended by Anderson.

Brayne was appointed on 14 November 1938 by a letter from the chief secretary to the Government of Punjab to the effect that Anderson had been unable to complete the inquiry against Inder Mohan and that its completion had been entrusted to Brayne.

Upon being appointed, Brayne's conduct reflected the nefarious agenda that was assigned to him. He immediately

[1]Ibid.

addressed a letter, dated 17 November 1938, to Inder Mohan, informing him that the inquiry, or at least a part of it, would have to be completed in Multan, and asking Inder Mohan for the earliest date on which he could meet Brayne there. In his letter, Brayne concluded that he did not expect that it would take more than, at most, one or two days. This was a complete give-away and it seemed that Brayne already knew what his final report would contain, even before he had studied all the papers, which he would have received only after his appointment on 14 November 1938. Anderson, who had conducted the initial inquiry in his report, had stated that he would require a week in Multan before he could come to a final conclusion. Brayne, who inherited this inquiry report from Anderson, and, at best, could have only read that report, came to an entirely different conclusion. He was a man in a hurry and would take only a few days to complete his inquiry.

Upon receipt of these communications, Inder Mohan said he understood that Anderson had completed the inquiry, and asked the chief secretary that he might be supplied with a copy of Anderson's report—or at least the portion of it in which it was said that his inquiry was incomplete—and a copy of the order of the Punjab government on the report. The conspiracy against Inder Mohan became even more apparent when the government refused to accede to this request and declined to give any further information. The Crown was in a hurry and did not want to accoutre Inder Mohan with any documentation that would enable him to defend his case.

Inder Mohan, who was never given access to the Anderson report, in his subsequent appeal[2] to the Privy Council, mentioned, 'The first paragraph of the confidential

---

[2]Author possesses a copy of the said document in his personal archives.

letter No. 7179-g-38/35792 dated 27th October, 1938 from the Chief Secretary Punjab Government to the Commissioner Rural Reconstruction Mr Anderson never said that he held a preliminary inquiry only. He also did not say that, "he was unable to complete the inquiry"...before he was transferred from Rawalpindi...' There was a deliberate attempt to misrepresent the findings of Anderson's report.

Inder Mohan also raised some pertinent objections to the appointment of Brayne to 'complete the preliminary inquiry' conducted by Anderson. In his petition to the Privy Council, he stated:

> Under the rule if the inquiry is incomplete the inquiring officer is to stay his hand and not to record his findings on the charges, but if after considering all the evidence as Mr. Anderson did, he finds the charges unproved, such findings in my submission, operates as an acquittal and the officer cannot be subject to another inquiry. The proceedings under the rule are exhausted and nothing more remains to be done. The regular and formal inquiry under the rule cannot be treated by the government as a preliminary inquiry... If such was not the case there would be no end to inquiries under the rules and Your Majesty's servants would always be under the fear of being harassed.[3]

A Biased Approach

As Inder Mohan was posted in Lyallpur, he addressed a letter to Brayne on 24 November 1938, saying that he might not be called to attend the inquiry until after Christmas, as

---

[3]Ibid.

he was to undertake a tour. However, Brayne continued to show his indolence and did not hearken to what appeared to be a reasonable request. In fact, he impetuously replied that his own engagements prevented him from dealing with the inquiry during the first half of January. He insisted that Inder Mohan meet him in Multan on the morning of 10 December 1939, and expressed the view that he could finish everything before the mail train left on Sunday afternoon, the next day, for Lahore. As if in a further display of effrontery, he subsequently, by letter and a telegram, asked Inder Mohan to meet him on the ninth of the month instead of on the tenth, as he desired to catch the mail train to Lahore on the tenth.

Not only was Brayne hell-bent on curtailing time but also insistent to make the inquiry even more partisan and tendentious. By a letter dated 29 November 1938, Brayne informed Inder Mohan that he proposed to examine various other documents in Multan and also indicated the classes of documents which he proposed to examine and the reasons why he was proposing to examine them. However, he refused to refer or allude to Anderson's report in any of these communications, as he had no intentions to share that report with Inder Mohan. Brayne would later take the stance[4] that these letters adequately apprised Inder Mohan of Brayne's mind. If anything, it certainly would have cautioned anybody of Brayne's biased state of mind.

Inder Mohan recorded in his appeal to the Privy Council:

> I was at Sheikhpura up till December 6, 1938 and reached Sargodha on the 7th. Meanwhile schools had

[4]As recorded in the Privy Council decision; 'High Commissioner of India and High Commissioner of Pakistan v I.M. Lall' before the Privy Council reported in 1948 Law Reports 75 IA 225.

started closing and my children had to come home. My sons were returning from Dehradun and I met them at Sheikhpura on 27th November. My daughters came from Dalhousie convent and I arranged to receive them at Lahore on 5th December. It would be seen that I had not only the worry of work and inquiry but to these added the worry of looking after the children returning from their schools.

I proceeded to Sargodha on the 7th December and took up a murder case. I was unable to complete it. On the 8th after court hours, I left by car for Lahore in order to catch the night train for Multan. It may be recalled that I had to meet Mr Brayne on that date and on the 12th, I had to take up the case I had to leave incomplete. I worked there up till the 17th. 18th was a Sunday. On the 21st I was working at Jhang. These facts are absolutely true and tell their story. I leave it to Your Majesty to decide how far in these circumstances I had been given a reasonable opportunity to defend myself.

[...] The significant fact to be noticed about these proceeds is that so far, I and Mr. Brayne had not met and the only facility that Mr. Brayne had given me was to advance the date of hearing one day in response to my request for postponement of the inquiry to a date after Christmas. The other favour that he was pleased to show me was to dispense with my presence at Multan on the 7th and 8th of December although he had been clearly informed by the Government that I wanted to be present in person at the inquiry.[5]

---

[5]Author possesses a copy of the said document in his personal archives.

Not only was Inder Mohan summoned at short notice, Brayne himself reached Multan on 7 December 1938, conducting his own inquiry behind Inder Mohan's back. To add to the insult, he appointed Chaman Lall on special duty to assist him in his inquiry. The person on whose complaint the inquiry was started, and who according to Inder Mohan, was his 'principal enemy', was appointed by Brayne as his assistant. In his petition before the Privy Council, Inder Mohan noted that the undue benefit of doubt was being accorded to Chaman Lall. In his discussion on one of the charges, he stated:

> In his note, Chaman Lall had not mentioned that the vacancy did not exist. This, Mr. Brayne regarded as 'obviously a genuine error'. Why 'obviously' and why an 'error' and why 'genuine'? Is there anything on the record to support such a finding? Is such a finding justified by the previous record of Chaman Lall? Is it supported by Mr. Brayne's own finding that 'Chaman Lall is not being regarded by me as a thoroughly reliable person'?[6]

About the presence of Brayne in Multan on 7 and 8 December, Inder Mohan submitted to the Privy Council that it was on these dates that Brayne collected more papers in an effort to crystallize the case against Inder Mohan. He complained that a 'court' (as Brayne would call his position while conducting the inquiry), which evaluates papers, should not be the one collecting them as well. Brayne was further accused of collecting a few documents and rejecting others as he deemed fit, without giving Inder Mohan an opportunity to respond. 'At the inquiry, evidence thus collected is judged by an authority different from the authority that collected it,' wrote Inder Mohan in his complaint. About

---

[6]Ibid.

Brayne, he said: '...if I had been given an opportunity Mr. Brayne would have been my first witness. I would have examined him about the documents that he had collected, the suspension of Chaman Lall, his proceedings in Multan and cognate matters, including his friendship with the Chief Justice.' Making a direct allegation against Brayne and how he collaborated with Chaman Lall, the petition also noted:

> The Chief Justice had received an anonymous application which internal evidence shows was written at the instigation of Chaman Lall. It contains a reference to my remarks in the character roll of some of the clerks. These remarks were confidential and the rolls were in the custody of L. Chaman Lall. He had the anonymous letter written and it is he who subsequently gave the explanation which puzzled Mr. Brayne so much.[7]

The reference to the 'puzzled Mr. Brayne' was a direct dig at the findings in his report and how he himself created evidence to use against Inder Mohan.

Meetings and Discussions

Inder Mohan met Brayne on 9 December 1938 in Multan. It was during this meeting that Brayne put several new documents before Inder Mohan and expected him to respond. He constantly reminded Inder Mohan of the paucity of time that he had in undertaking this inquiry. Inder Mohan, however, persisted with his stand that he considered Anderson's inquiry complete, asked for a copy of Anderson's report and requested for adequate time to study these documents before he was

---

[7]Ibid.

interviewed. He simply could not understand why Anderson's inquiry report was not being treated as the final report.

Under such circumstances, the interview conducted by Brayne was a short one. Refusing to supply a copy of Anderson's report, he asked Inder Mohan to put his representations in writing by 19 December and be present for another meeting on 20 December, this time in Lahore. Brayne did not interview anybody in Multan, so it was unclear why he had called for a meeting there in the first place.

As Inder Mohan persisted with his demand for papers, Brayne finally heeded and supplied him with copies of relevant parts of the new documents before their next meeting. Inder Mohan was given documents that were already on record; there were also several new documents, which included a list of 42-character rolls, in which entries had been made by Inder Mohan in 1936 and 1937.

Time was short, as Inder Mohan had to study these papers and prepare his defence within the next few days. Being a man determined to prove his innocence, he burnt the midnight oil. In his heart of hearts, he knew he was fighting a losing battle, but he was determined to fight.

On 18 December, Inder Mohan sent to Brayne his submissions in writing in regard to the latter's inquiry, in which he again made it abundantly clear that he did not understand what was happening, what the further documents were for—none of it was mentioned in the charge sheet.

Under these circumstances, Inder Mohan met Brayne again at Lahore on 20 December. Unlike on the previous occasion, this interview lasted a considerable length of time. According to Brayne's own note, which was produced as evidence in court, it was in this meeting that Brayne for the first time explained the relevance of the new documents to Inder Mohan and the reasons for which he was looking at them. Of course, one could only understand the relevance of these documents if one had the benefit of Anderson's report, a benefit that Inder Mohan did not have.

However, Inder Mohan persisted that unless he was given a copy of Anderson's report and the government orders passed thereafter, he would not consider himself to have been given an adequate opportunity of defending himself as provided by Rule 55, Civil Services (Classification, Control and Appeal) Rules. Inder Mohan also asked for certain other documents and requested that only thereafter could he appropriately address Brayne about the case.

After the second meeting, Brayne permitted Inder Mohan to place a written memorandum on the case by 26 December, which was duly complied by Inder Mohan. On 30 December, both Brayne and Inder Mohan met again. However, this time Brayne was encumbered, as he had yet not received the additional written memorandum from Inder Mohan. Inder Mohan requested for the meeting to be adjourned, as he expressed the desire to address Brayne again personally after he had read the written memorandum. The date of 2 January 1939 was fixed for this purpose, and according to Brayne's representation, Inder Mohan managed to say all that he wanted to regarding the case. What Brayne missed was that, in his representation, Inder Mohan clearly mentioned the fact that he never got an opportunity to read Anderson's report and, whilst that was a handicap in itself, additionally, without the report, he could not decipher the relevance of many documents that were subsequently given to him.

I will now deal with the ...

Brayne's Report.

Part III.

97. After stating the charges Mr. Brayne commences his report under the heading "Diary of Events". He states he discovered these facts from "papers and Mr.Lall's statements". My submission is that he suppressed very important dates that I had given to him in writing and he concealed from me the papers from which he got dates for his "Diary of Events". His very first date 5th of June is wrong and suggests a very misleading inference. Altogether he mentions 50 dates. Of these 22 dates relate to documents of which I had no knowledge whatever. Some of these documents were not cited as evidence under any charge. I was not given copies of them. They were not produced as evidence by any body in my presence. Their genuineness is not established. Of the rest I was given copies of 14 only. I do not know who gave information to Mr.Brayne of these documents. It is not known if these documents came from proper custody. No one was examined as a witness in my presence to prove the contents of these documents. I will urge my detailed objections against each document.

5th June 1935. I did not take over charge on this date. The

Excerpt from the Privy Council appeal document
Source: The British Library

Verdict

On 24 January 1939, Brayne completed his inquiry and report. The report was venomous. He went to the extent of stating that he was not content with merely accepting Inder Mohan's plea of guilt to the charges of nepotism, but went into the details and surrounding circumstances at great length, and found that the nepotism was 'complete and deliberate'. Inder Mohan described Brayne's inquiry report as not being just partial but also one that indulged in denigration. He commented:

In my statement before Mr Anderson I had stated that I would accept any punishment that the Government is pleased to award. Such a statement did not suit Mr Brayne and therefore in the report he represented me in the worst possible colour. He talks of Mr Lall regarding 'nepotism as harmless' and 'easing my domestic conscience' and having 'no sense of inquisitiveness' etc. etc. I submit to Your Majesty Mr Brayne has indulged in cheap sneer.[8]

I submit the following repres-entation for the just and sympathetic consideration of the Government of India.

1. The inquiry against me was held under rule 55 of the Classification Rules made by the Secretary of State for India under section 96 of the old Government of India Act. This rule contains inter alia;

(a) That allegations on which it is proposed to take action should be stated in the form of charge or charges.

(b) That the officer should be informed in writing of the grounds on which each charge is based i.e. each charge should state the evidence on which it is founded.

In view of these precise provisions it is necessary that the inquiry should be confined to the language of the charge or charges and the evidence mentioned under each charge. Evidence on one charge should not be treated as evidence on any other charge; and secondly the charges should state in precise language the allegation contained in them. In other words the officer should receive full information from the language of

First page of I.M. Lall's defence against the inquiry
Source: National Archives of India

[8]Ibid.

Inder Mohan also questioned the moral efficacy of the officials holding the inquiry. He stated:

> Moreover, I submit respectfully, my judges are in this matter no better than myself and Mr Brayne. Sir Henry Clarke whose recommendation I do not know was the Governor. He was an I.C.S officer like myself and Mr Brayne. He had twice my service and many times my experience. He employs his own son-in-law as his military secretary. I employed my wife's nephew as a petty clerk. What is nepotism in me is nepotism in the Governor. The principle is the same and what is sauce for the goose is sauce for the gander also.
>
> Your Majesty's Secretary of State for India will report to you all the facts of this case, I refer to the case of Mr. Justice Beckett of the Lahore High Court, Mr. Beckett has now been appointed a permanent Judge of Lahore High Court... Six months or so before, he had been superseded. It was all manoeuvred by the Chief Justice. Your Majesty will see that in this matter the head of the ICS in the province, and the head of my department, are in the same boat with me. Their indignation at my 'nepotism' is hardly justified.[9]

As regards the charges of vindictiveness, Brayne again went into the details and surrounding circumstances and found that the charges were fully proved. He had reached this conclusion without formally examining Chaman Lall or the other six witnesses whom Inder Mohan had accused of victimization. Of course, there was no question of giving Inder Mohan any opportunity of hearing their testimony or cross-examining them. Inder Mohan later complained to the Privy Council:

---

[9]Ibid.

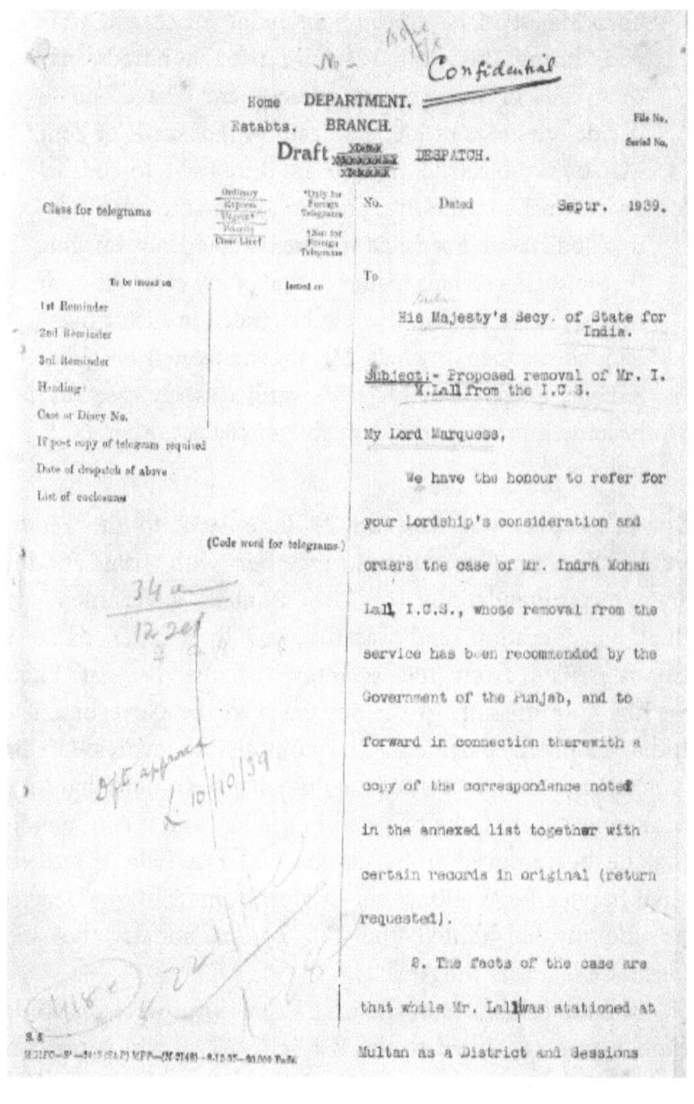

Confidential

Home DEPARTMENT.
Estabts. BRANCH.
Draft DESPATCH.

File No.
Serial No.

Class for telegrams

No. Dated Septr. 1939.

To be issued on — Issued on

1st Reminder
2nd Reminder
3rd Reminder
Heading:
Case or Diary No.
If post copy of telegram required
Date of despatch of above
List of enclosures

(Code word for telegrams)

To

His Majesty's Secy. of State for India.

Subject:- Proposed removal of Mr. I. M. Lall from the I.C.S.

My Lord Marquess,

We have the honour to refer for your Lordship's consideration and orders the case of Mr. Indra Mohan Lall, I.C.S., whose removal from the service has been recommended by the Government of the Punjab, and to forward in connection therewith a copy of the correspondence noted in the annexed list together with certain records in original (return requested).

2. The facts of the case are that while Mr. Lall was stationed at Multan as a District and Sessions

Letter to Lord Marques, Secretary of State, suggesting the removal of I.M. Lall from the ICS

Source: National Archives of India

> Your Majesty, I have been your Judge for several years and during this period I have tried hundreds, nay thousands of very serious cases where I have had to decide questions of life and death of thousands of Your Majesty's subjects. I have been thus used to judicial procedures and the interpretation of statutes and rules in a judicial and sensible manner. I could not imagine that in such a serious matter as that of my career as Your Majesty's civil servant I would be treated in such a high-handed manner in which Mr. Brayne treated me. I am anxious to get Your Majesty's verdict as my case may become a precedent and might thus affect other I.C.S. officers.[10]

Brayne's report was sent on 21 June 1939 to the Federal Public Service Commission, together with some finding and recommendations of the Punjab government for their consideration, and was followed by a letter, dated 31 August 1939, from the secretary of the Federal Public Service Commission to the secretary to the Government of India, Home Department. The commission expressed their concurrence in the views of the Punjab government that Inder Mohan was unfit to be retained in the ICS and recommended that he be removed from service under Article 353 of the Civil Service Regulations, but in view of his 17 years' service, he should be granted the full compassionate allowance permissible under the Article.

The material facts in the case for removal were that Inder Mohan was appointed to the ICS in 1922, at which point he signed a covenant that contained the principal terms of his

[10]Ibid.

employment. The covenant recited that the Secretary of State in Council had appointed Inder Mohan 'to serve His Majesty as a member of the Civil Service of India...such service to continue during the pleasure of His Majesty, his heirs and successors, to be signified under the hand of the Secretary of State for India'.[11] It is the interpretation of this covenant that came into issue, and indeed, galvanized me to choose the title of this book.

In the Gazette of 10 August 1940, there appeared a notification over the signature of the chief secretary, Punjab government, to the effect that 'His Majesty's Secretary of State for India has directed the removal of Mr. I. M. Lall from the Indian Civil Service with effect from the 4th June, 1940'. By a letter dated 10 August 1940, Inder Mohan was informed by the Punjab government of his removal and was given a copy of the letter no. F 128/39-S, dated 31 August, 1939 from the Federal Public Service Commission, which advised that I.M. Lall be removed from service. In a letter to the Secretary of State referenced in the petition to the Privy Council, the Home Department recommended:

> The Provincial Government recommends that in view of the length of his service Mr. Lall may be granted the maximum compassionate allowance admissible under art 353 of the Civil Service Regulations, i.e., he may be given two thirds of the pension admissible to him if he were to retire on medical certificate. The Honourable Chief Justice, who has been consulted, concurs in these recommendations of the Provincial Government.
>
> After a careful consideration of all the circumstances

[11]Ibid.

of the case, we are in complete agreement with the view taken in this case by the Provincial Government and the Federal P.C.C. and the facts of the case leave no room for doubt as to the unfitness of Mr Lall for further retention in the service. Therefore, support the recommendation of the Government of the Punjab that Mr. Lall be removed from the Indian Civil Service and that he may be granted the maximum compassionate allowance admissible under article 353-0.3.R.

7

Aftermath of the Dismissal (1939-44)

The findings of Brayne's report and the subsequent actions initiated by the government fell like a tonne of bricks on the Lall household. It was not unexpected, yet there had been hope that perhaps the powers to be would see reason. It was not to be.

However, Inder Mohan was relentless and remained committed in his attempts to secure copies of the reports of both Anderson and Brayne, and make personal representations to the authorities. In June 1939, he pressed for an interview with the governor of Punjab and on 16 June, he repeated his request for the copies of the report. This interview was, however, not granted on the ground that his case had been passed to a higher authority. On 23 June 1939, Inder Mohan requested that if the authority to decide his case was the Secretary of State, he should be permitted to place his side of the case before the latter in person and that he might be granted facilities for that purpose. On 26 June, he was told that if he had representations to make, they could be addressed to the Governor General in the form of a memorial under the rules relating to the submission of memorials.

Dissatisfied with the responses, in the spring of 1940, Inder Mohan proceeded to London to make a representation in person at the India office. By then, Britain had already declared war on Nazi Germany. His principal grievance was that at no time, before his removal from service, was he allowed to see the reports of either Anderson or Brayne, nor was he informed that the Punjab government or the Federal Public Service Commission or the Government of India or the Secretary of State were proposing on the basis of those reports to remove him from the service. He had only received the general invitation to show cause against possible dismissal (amongst other possible punishments) included at the end of the charges originally served against him. But he had not been given an opportunity to show cause against dismissal, after it had passed from being a possible punishment to the punishment proposed and recommended. At no time was he given an opportunity, before dismissal, of making representations against the accuracy of facts found by Anderson or Brayne in their reports or against the adverse deductions drawn against him, particularly by Brayne.

In his appeal, Inder Mohan noted:

> I wish I had been heard by the Governor after a copy of the report had been made available to me, or by the F.P.S.C., or the Government of India, or even by Your Majesty's Secretary of State for India. I was denied hearing at all stages and the result has been that perverse findings of Mr. Brayne have been accepted by the Secretary of State. I submit to Your Majesty with full sense of responsibility that all this has happened because I was an ICS officer.[1]

---

[1]Author possesses a copy of the said document in his personal archives.

Inder Mohan's Suit

After Inder Mohan had been notified of his removal, he additionally questioned the authority under which the Secretary of State had purported to order his removal. In a letter from the chief secretary to the Punjab government, he was informed on 19 March 1941, that the Secretary of State had not disclosed the authority under which he was acting, but the attention of Inder Mohan was drawn to Rule 50, Civil Services (Classification, Control and Appeal) Rules read in conjunction with sub-section (2) of Section 240 of the Government of India Act, 1935. Section 240 of the Government of India Act, 1935, reads as follows:

1. Except as expressly provided by this Act, every person who is a member of a civil service of the Crown in India, or holds any civil post under the Crown in India, holds office during His Majesty's pleasure.
2. No such person as aforesaid shall be dismissed from the service of His Majesty by any authority subordinate to that by which he was appointed.[2]

Since Inder Mohan was not satisfied with this reply and made inquiries with the Secretary of State himself, a further letter dated 6 October 1941 was issued to him by which he was informed through the Punjab government that in removing him from the ICS, 'the Secretary of State acted on behalf of His Majesty in exercise of the rights of the Crown to dismiss its servants at pleasure.' The powers that be at the time considered ICS officers as servants who were appointed and dismissed at the pleasure of the Crown.

---

[2]'Chapter II, Civil Services, General Provisions', Government of India Act, 1935, p. 144, https://tinyurl.com/yrzmmevx. Accessed on 7 August 2023.

For now, these were difficult times in the Lall household. There were eight children, with the eldest, Tilak, only 15 years old, and Jogi under one. Inder Mohan could ill-afford their upbringing and was not going to take this decision lying down. To manage the finances, Inder Mohan joined a Tata company as a consultant.

On 20 July 1942, he instituted a suit against the Secretary of State for India, challenging the validity of the order dated 10 August 1940, which removed him from the ICS. The suit was instituted in the court of Lala Tara Chand Aggarwal, sub-judge, first class, Lahore, seeking (1) a declaration that the order of removal was ultra vires of the Secretary of State; (2) that the order was not passed in accordance with due process of law and was wrongful, illegal and of no consequence whatever; (3) that he was still a member of the ICS, and had a right to continue in it, and to hold the office from which he was removed by the illegal order of the Secretary of State; and (4) that as a member of the ICS, he was entitled to all rights secured to him by the covenant and rules and regulations issued from time to time by the appropriate authority.

This was the time when the Second World War as well as the Indian nationalist movement were at their peak. The INC had demanded independence before it would help Britain in the war effort. In August 1942, the Congress announced the Quit India Movement, asking Britain to leave India.

Meanwhile, Lala Tara Chand Aggarwal decided to limit his decision as to 'whether the Secretary of State had authority to remove the plaintiff from the Indian Civil Service, even if the enquiries were illegal or ultra vires.'[3] Since both parties to

---

[3]'I.M. Lall v Secretary of State', High Court of Lahore, 27 March 1944, MANU/LA/0109/1944.

the suit wanted it to be tried by the Lahore High Court, an application was accordingly made for transfer on the grounds that novel points of law, of considerable difficulty, dealing with the interpretation of the Government of India Act, 1935, were likely to be involved. The reason for seeking the transfer was also that oral evidence was not going to be considerable and since the matter would not rest with the decision of the first and original court, a transfer to the High Court would avoid the probability of a multiplicity of appeals and would be convenient for both parties.

The suit was then set down for trial before a single judge of the High Court. However, the High Court considered that, as there was a likelihood of a Letters Patent Appeal in a matter of great importance, the case should be heard by a Division Bench, comprising two judges. Accordingly, papers were laid before the Chief Justice, who directed that the suit be heard by a Division Bench as a court of first instance. The Division Bench framed the following additional issues that would be decided by the court:

1. Did the Secretary of State have authority to remove Inder Mohan from the ICS?
2. Was it incumbent on the Secretary of State to hold an inquiry before making an order removing Inder Mohan from service?
3. If so, what should be the nature of such an inquiry?
4. Was Inder Mohan not given adequate opportunity of defending himself as contemplated in Rule 55, Civil Services (Classification, Control and Appeal) Rules? If not, what is the effect?
5. Was Inder Mohan not given a reasonable opportunity of giving show cause as laid down in section 240(3) of

the Government of India Act, 1935? If not, what is the effect?

6. Is the [Division Bench] Court entitled to determine the question whether the opportunity given was reasonable or not?
7. Did Brayne not conduct the inquiry bona fide? If not, what is the effect?

The matter was finally decided by Justice Ram Lall and Abdul Rashid of a Division Bench of the Lahore High Court. The decision of the court was handed down on 27 March 1944, in *I.M. Lall v Secretary of State*[4]. On the preliminary issue before the Privy Council, the High Court came to the conclusion that Inder Mohan could not be removed from office until he had been given a reasonable opportunity of showing cause. This determination also governed the decision of the court on Issue No. 2, with the court holding that it was incumbent on the Secretary of State to hold an inquiry before making an order removing Inder Mohan from service.

On the first issue, the High Court held that the Secretary of State did indeed have the authority to remove Inder Mohan from the ICS, it being subject to holding an inquiry and him having been given a reasonable opportunity to show cause. On Issue No. 3, it decided that the legal obligation would be adequately complied with provided that the person concerned knew all the charges against him, and an inquiry was held in such a manner that he had reasonable opportunity to defend himself and was not prejudiced against or misled in the matter of his defence. On Issue No. 4 and 5, the High Court came to the conclusion that on the facts of the case,

---

[4]Ibid.

the inquiry had not been conducted by Brayne in accordance with the legal requirements. On Issue No. 6, the court held that a court should get into the issue and determine whether the opportunity given to Inder Mohan was reasonable. On Issue No. 7, the court found that Brayne had not conducted the inquiry in accordance with legal requirements and the conduct of the inquiry could not be regarded as bona fide.

Resultantly, the High Court decided all the issues in favour of Inder Mohan and made a declaration that the order of his removal was 'wrongful, void, illegal and inoperative and that he still remained a member of the Indian Civil Service'. As Inder Mohan had succeeded substantially in this suit, the court directed the Secretary of State to pay all costs incurred by Inder Mohan.

At the request of the Crown, the High Court also gave a certificate to the effect that the case involved substantial questions of law as to the interpretation of the Government of India Act of 1935 and accordingly it was a case fit for appeal in the Federal Court.[5]

Appeal

The Secretary of State for India appealed the decision of the Division Bench to the Federal Court. The Federal Court, which heard the appeal, comprised a bench of Sir Patrick Spens, Chief Justice Sir S. Varadachariar and Sir Muhammad

[5]While researching the case, the author also discovered an anecdotal side issue. The counsel who was opposing Inder Mohan was S.M. Sikri, who went on to become the Chief Justice of India. He was the first lawyer to be directly elevated to the Supreme Court in 1964. Prior to that, he was appointed as the Advocate General of Punjab.

IN THE FEDERAL COURT.

Civil Appeal No. XII of 1944.

(*Appellate Jurisdiction.*)

ON APPEAL FROM THE HIGH COURT OF JUDICATURE AT LAHORE.

THE SECRETARY OF STATE FOR INDIA ... *Appellant,*

versus

I. M. LALL ... ... *Respondent.*

Counsel for the Appellant: Mr. N. P. Engineer (with Mr. S. M. Sikri), instructed by Mr. K. Y. Bhandarkar, Agent.

Respondent in person, instructed by Mr. Naunit Lal, Agent.

JUDGMENT.

SPENS, *C.J.*—This is an appeal by the Secretary of State for India in a suit instituted by the respondent, Mr. I. M. Lall who was a senior member of the Indian Civil Service in the year 1940, when the Secretary of State for India purported to remove him from the service. Mr. Lall's suit was originally commenced in the Court of the Sub-Judge, First Class, Lahore. It was later transferred to the High Court for hearing and was finally heard by a Division Bench of the High Court (Abdul Rashid and Ram Lall JJ.). On the 27th March, 1944, the High Court made a decree in Mr. Lall's favour declaring that the order made in the year 1940 for the removal of Mr. Lall from the Indian Civil Service with effect from the 4th June, 1940, was wrongful, void, illegal and inoperative, and that Mr. Lall was still a member of the Indian Civil Service. At the time the learned Judges made this order they added a note to their judgment that several substantial questions of law as to the interpretation of the Government of India Act, 1935, were involved in the case, and they accordingly certified that it was a fit case for appeal to the Federal Court. Hence this appeal. It was suggested by Mr. Lall that the above certificate was not in proper form to comply with s. 205 of the Constitution Act, 1935. We were wholly unable to accept any such contention. The intention of the learned Judges is quite plain. No particular form of certificate is required.

The material facts can be summarised as follows:—

Mr. Lall was appointed to the Indian Civil Service in the year 1922, and on the 1st September in that year entered into a covenant with the Secretary of State in Council. The covenant recited that the Secretary of State in Council had appointed Mr. Lall "to serve His Majesty as a member of the Civil Service of India........ such service to continue during the pleasure of His Majesty. His

Opening page of the Federal Court judgment delivered by Chief Justice Sir Patrick Spens and Sir Muhammad Zafrulla Khan (concurring) and Sir S. Varadachariar (dissenting) in the cases titled 'The Secretary of State for India v I.M. Lall'

Source: National Archives of India

Zafrullah Khan. The Federal Court had been established by the British on 1 October 1937, with original appellate and advisory jurisdiction. The seat of the court was the Chamber of Princes in Parliament building in Delhi. It functioned until the establishment of the Supreme Court of India on 28 January 1950, two days after India was declared a republic. Sir Patrick Spens was the Chief Justice of the Federal Court from 7 June 1943 to 14 August 1947. He hailed from the Inner Temple. Sir S. Varadachariar was also the acting Chief Justice of the Federal Court prior to the appointment of Sir Patrick Spens between the period 25 April 1943 and 7 June 1943. Muhammad Zafarullah Khan was appointed a judge of the Federal Court in September 1941. In 1954, he went on to become a judge at the International Court of Justice (ICJ) in The Hague, a position he held until 1961.

The Federal Court, by a majority decision (with Sir Patrick Spens, Chief Justice, and Sir Muhammad Zafrullah Khan concurring and Sir S. Varadachariar dissenting) dated 4 May 1945, held that when it is proposed to dismiss or lower a civil servant in rank, he should be given a reasonable opportunity of providing show cause against the proposal. The civil servant is required to be told and given an opportunity to put his case against the proposed action, and that opportunity has to be a reasonable one. Not only is the civil servant required to be notified of the action proposed, but also the grounds on which the authority is proposing that action, and that the person concerned must then be given reasonable time to make his representations against the proposed action.

The Federal Court further held that in all cases where there is an inquiry and, as a result thereof, some authority definitely proposes dismissal or reduction in rank, the person concerned has to be told in full, or adequately summarized form, the results of that inquiry and the findings of the inquiring officer, and be given an opportunity of giving show cause with the information stating why he should not suffer the proposed dismissal or reduction of rank. While the tenure of the office, the court held, is at His Majesty's pleasure and the power of dismissal is at the will of His Majesty, the law imposes certain statutory obligations to be carried out before dismissal is affected, breach of which will give to the person adversely affected a cause to come to court.

After setting down the law, the majority decision of the Federal Court concluded that as per the facts of the case, it was clear that no such opportunity has been given to Inder Mohan despite his repeated efforts to be informed of the results of Anderson's and Brayne's inquiries and to make representations on their reports. No information had been given to him regarding the proposals of the Punjab government or of the Federal Public Service Commission or of the Government of India stating that he should be dismissed. The court held that Inder Mohan had not been given an 'adequate opportunity of defending himself'. Based on this decision, the Federal Court varied the decree: '[...] the order removing the plaintiff from office was wrongful, void, illegal and inoperative and that the plaintiff is still a member of the Indian Civil Service shall be substituted by a declaration that the plaintiff Mr. I.M. Lall was wrongfully dismissed from the Indian Civil Service on June 4, 1940'. The Federal Court remitted the suit to the High Court for assessment of damages. S.M. Sikri represented the State before the Federal Court.

These two decisions of the Division Bench of the Lahore High Court and the Federal Court of India severely dented the might of the British empire. Inder Mohan was but a subject of the Empire and the Crown. David had defeated the Goliath.

Having won the case in two courts, Inder Mohan hoped that his ordeals had come to an end, but it was not to be. More was to follow.

Rumours of Partition

On 7 May 1945, only a few days after the Federal Court's decision, Germany surrendered, bringing an end to the Second World War. British resources were fully stretched after the war. Britain became a flailing world power and was going bankrupt. In July 1945, Winston Churchill's government lost the general election, and the Labour Party came to power in an unexpected victory.

Britain was getting ready to leave the shores of India. Simultaneously, communal tensions between Hindus and Muslims were rising. Communal clashes between Hindus and Muslims became frequent, and talks about partition of India had started almost a year before the actual event in August 1947. 16 August 1946 and the week that ensued, exactly a year before Partition, was termed 'the week of the long knives'[6] when rioting in Calcutta (now Kolkata) left over 4,000 dead and over a 100,000 homeless.[7]

During the war, Britain had called upon its colonies for manpower. Over 2.3 million Indian soldiers were recruited and

---

[6]Sengupta, Debjani, 'A City Feeding on Itself: Testimonies and Histories of "Direct Action' Day", *Sarai Reader*, Vol. 6 (Turbulence), https://tinyurl.com/5n8khb9j. Accessed on 6 December 2023.

[7]Burrows, Frederick, 'Report to Viceroy Lord Wavell' *The British Library*, 1946.

inducted into the war.[8] All this happened on the promise that Britain would hand over political power in exchange for this cooperation. In February 1947, Prime Minister (PM) of Britain Clement Attlee announced Britain's intention to leave India. Lord Louis Francis Albert Victor Mountbatten was appointed as the last viceroy of India. Mountbatten, referred to by many as Dickie Mountbatten, was the great-grandson of Queen Victoria, the British monarch who had given herself the title of Empress of India, though she never set foot on India.

On 3 March 1947, Hindu and Sikh leaders met in Lahore, where they vowed to oppose the establishment of Pakistan. On 4 March, Hindu and Sikh students came on the streets to protest. Communal clashes broke out in different parts of Lahore. By the evening, communal violence broke out in Amritsar and, on March 5, in Multan and Rawalpindi. On 5 March 1947, Sir Evan Jenkins imposed Governor's Rule after the Muslim League failed to convince him that it had a stable majority in the Punjab Assembly. Punjab remained under Governor's Rule until power was handed over to the Pakistani and Indian governments on 14 and 15 August, respectively.

Lord Louis Mountbatten announced the Partition plan on 3 June 1947, declaring that the British had decided to transfer power to the Indian and Pakistani governments by mid-August 1947. Though his appointment was till June 1948, he advanced the date for Britain to leave India by 10 months. The announcement resulted in a further increase in violence as uncertainty over the future triggered the greatest forced migration in history. The partition of Punjab proved to be

[8]'India and the Commonwealth War Graves Commission', *Commonwealth War Grave Commissions*, http://tinyurl.com/5b3u87zj. Accessed on 13 December 2023.

one of the most violent in the history of humankind. Being Hindus, Inder Mohan's family was caught in the midst of it all in Lahore.

The Second World War may have ended, but on Inder Mohan's front, the war was still on. Despite being fully stretched on all fronts, the Crown instructed the Secretary of State for India to appeal the decision of the Federal Court to the Privy Council. The Judicial Committee of the Privy Council was the highest court of appeal for some of the British territories and Commonwealth countries. Established on 13 August 1833, it acted as the court of last resort for the entire British Empire. India retained the right of appeal from the Federal Court of India to the Privy Council after the establishment of the Dominion of India. Following the replacement of the Federal Court with the Supreme Court of India in January 1950, the Abolition of Privy Council Jurisdiction Act, 1949 came into effect, ending the right of appeal to the Judicial Committee of the Privy Council.

Upon being served with the appeal papers, Inder Mohan immediately started to contact counsels in Britain to represent him. However, none were willing to come forward to represent him against the Crown. Inder Mohan had no option but to travel to London to either find a counsel or represent himself. By now, it was almost certain that India would be free of British rule. The writing was also on the wall that this departure of the British was not going to be a smooth one. Inder Mohan had no option but to leave for London in the midst of all this. He had to leave early, as it took a three-week-long sea voyage to reach London. He needed to reach in time to prepare his case before the Privy Council and find himself a counsel to represent him.

8

Tears of Blood: Partition

In early 1947, undivided Punjab was ruled by a coalition ministry of Unionists, Sikhs and the Congress party members headed by the Unionist leader, Sir Khizar Hayat Tiwana. The elections in 1946 had given the Muslim League 75 of the 175 seats.[1] As it was not enough for them to form the government, they had formed a coalition. On 20 February 1947, the British government had announced their decision to withdraw from India by June 1948. This date was later advanced. The announcement had increased the political ferment in Punjab. The Muslim League's efforts to wield power over Punjab, the linchpin province of its envisioned future Pakistan, became more urgent. The Unionist Party's proximity to and patronage by the British Indian administration and the British Indian Army had been the main source of its power and legitimacy in Punjab. Now that the British had definitely decided to withdraw from the region and effectively ditch their chief sub-continental ally of many decades, the Unionist Party immediately and swiftly lost its prestige.

On 2 March 1947, Sir Hayat finally decided to resign, and in the succeeding few days, Punjab experienced widespread

---

[1]Gosain, Renu, 'The Muslim Politics in Undivided Punjab: Khizr–Jinnah Tussle', *Asian Resonance*, Vol. 4, No. 3, July 2015, https://tinyurl.com/ys8dakdt. Accessed on 7 August 2023.

urban and rural outbreaks of violence. Upon the resignation of Sir Hayat, the Muslim League attempted to seize power not by consensus but by force. Within weeks, the violence spread from cities to the countryside and took on the sinister tone of ethnic cleansing.

Meanwhile, in Inder Mohan's household, no one had quite realized the enormity of what was going on. On the night of 3 March 1947, a large meeting was held in Lahore. It was a non-Muslim meeting during which calls for violence were made. It was held in an open field in the heart of the town. Fiery speeches in *maidans* and popular gathering places were becoming a norm for politicians to further their agendas. Communalism was becoming the pathway to garner support. These always resulted in igniting hatred against another community, resulting in rioting and killing. Facts intertwined with rumours of one community having victimized the other would result in violent responses. This meeting, essentially for the Hindu community, was no exception. Fiery speeches were made at the meeting. Hindus and Sikhs decided to fight Partition, as they did not want to lose their homes. Inder Mohan's adventurous son Amar, out of sheer curiosity, attended this meeting.

The rhetoric of the speakers against the Muslim communities resulted in rioting the very next day. The riots in Lahore spread over the next few days to Multan, Rawalpindi, Amritsar and Jalandhar. In Lahore itself, the students of Dayal Singh College and DAV College, which were predominantly Hindu institutions, decided to take out a procession to oppose the formation of Pakistan. Such processions had become commonplace at the time. The Muslim community, in turn, would hold its own meetings, processions and rallies favouring Partition. Communities were being trained to become partisan and intolerant of each other.

Riot at the College

On 4 March, the procession of students from Dayal Singh College and DAV College entered GCUL, which is where Amar was studying at the time. The government college was built on top of a hill, and its gates led to the driveway. The procession entered the gates of the college, and some of the protesters went and broke one or two window panes. Slowly, the entire college premises turned into a war zone, compelling the principal, Patras Bokhari, a die-hard Muslim League supporter, to call the police.

The GCUL had an equal number of Hindu and Muslim students. The police parked themselves outside the entrance gate, came out of their vehicles and formed a cordon in front of the gate. However, there were about 2,000-odd students inside the college at the time and the policemen were no more than 50 in number. Initially, some policemen went inside the college to negotiate with the students and attempted to disperse the crowds. For the students, it was all fun and frolic, and nobody was taking it seriously. Some of the student leaders took the charge to negotiate with the police.

But discussions soon turned abusive. Things took a turn for the worse when some students started to pelt stones at the police personnel. The policemen did not have guns and were only armed with canes and sticks. To protect themselves, they started to retreat. Taking advantage of the situation, more students joined in pelting of stones. The policemen ran into their buses to take shelter and pulled down the wooden shutters on the bus windows. At the time, such wooden shutters were considered sufficiently secure, as skirmishes with the citizens were rare. Things were different now, and with the policemen on the run, the students had tasted blood, so they broke the shutters and started throwing stones inside the bus. Being outnumbered by the students, the policemen tried to hold on to their turbans, called *kullas* (hard caps), to protect their heads. However, they quickly realized that the buses were not sufficient shelter for them and were thus compelled to run out and seek shelter in the district judge's courtrooms nearby. The students started to run after the policemen.

As the situation worsened, word spread and an Englishman by the name of Williams reached the spot with a few policemen. Even these policemen were only armed with sticks. William himself was armed with a double barrel rifle. By now, students had moved out of the college and had started to congregate in a triangular garden outside. In an effort to disperse the crowds, William started to fire in the direction of the students. This resulted in further pandemonium, with students running in all directions. The policemen, realizing that the situation had reversed, also started venting their ire on the students by chasing and beating them with their batons.

For Amar, this was all one big adventure. Having taken military training courses as part of his curriculum, he guided his friends to lie flat on the ground should there be shooting in their direction. In jest, he said, 'Don't worry about dirtying your clothes, just lie flat on the ground.'

Fortunately, in the confusion, Amar and his friends were able to pick up their bicycles and rush home. Upon reaching home, Amar decided to regale his father Inder Mohan with the happenings of the morning. Far from being amused, Inder Mohan was horrified and, though he banned Amar from stepping out of the house, his own curiosity was piqued, and he set out in his Studebaker car to scout the situation for himself. After a while, he too returned. The deteriorating situation, far from being a deterrent, had whet his appetite to explore more.

So, after lunch, Inder Mohan, along with Dropadi, Amar and Pushpa, set out in the car for an exploratory trip around Lahore.

Amar recalls that from many places they could hear chants of *Jinnah Zindabad*. As they reached Sir Ganga Ram Hospital, they saw policemen standing with .303 rifles, the ones used in the First World War. The inspector was armed with a revolver. They were stopped and the inspector asked Inder Mohan as to what he was doing there. Inder Mohan responded that they had heard a lot of noise outside, so they had come to inspect. Amar would later narrate what the inspector had said, 'So you have come to see the fun? You, your wife, your daughter and your son, you've come to see the fun? You think this is all very funny?'

The conditions in Lahore were clearly neither conducive for Hindus nor safe. It was April 1947, and Inder Mohan was to travel to England to defend himself before the Privy Council soon. But he had to first find a way to keep his family safe.

Budh Singh Bindra was the senior superintendent of police (SSP) in Lahore at the time and a neighbour of the Lall family. The Bindras lived in the adjacent house and were like family to Inder Mohan and Dropadi.

The children of the Lall family and the Bindra family, which included Budh Singh and his wife Maan Kaur and their children Narinder, Bir Raminder, Avinash and Gyan Jotinder, grew up in each other's homes. Inder Mohan was assured by Budh Singh that the Lall family would be treated by him like his own and that he would ensure their well-being. On this assurance, Inder Mohan sailed to England in April 1947.

Partition in Lahore

SSP Budh Singh Bindra
Source: Singh family albums

By July 1947, being a senior officer in the police department, Budh Singh started receiving information that Lahore was likely to go to Pakistan. He accordingly sought a transfer to the city of Amritsar, which was likely to be in India. As Budh Singh started to make arrangements to move to Amritsar, he reached out to Dropadi and requested her to move with her family as well. He had made all arrangements for both families—the Bindras and the Lalls—to move to Amritsar. Dropadi, however, was having none of it. She held the view that Inder Mohan would return from England to Lahore, and she would await his return. With Tilak, the eldest son having left for America, Amar was the eldest amongst the male members; Budh Singh attempted to convince him as well. Clearly, the Lall family did not prognosticate the situation, and made the wrong decision of staying back in Lahore.

Budh Singh and his family departed for Amritsar in July 1947. Both the elders, Inder Mohan and Budh Singh, who wielded sufficient influence to ensure a safe passage for the family, had now left. Dropadi and the children stayed on in Lahore—a Hindu family in a Muslim-dominated area.

Between 15 and 17 August, there was great confusion about the actual boundaries between India and Pakistan. In fact, Lord Mountbatten, the last viceroy of India, who was in charge of Partition, did not disclose the final boundaries till two days after Partition. These boundaries were also hurriedly drawn up by Cyril Radcliffe, a British barrister, within five weeks. Radcliffe had never set foot in India before. This hurriedly-made-up border would decide the fate of over 400 million Indians. Many found themselves on the wrong side of the border suddenly. Lahore was awarded to Pakistan, which is where Inder Mohan's family home was.

It was on 15 August that the news anchor on the radio announced that the country had been divided into two parts, India and Pakistan. Pandit Jawaharlal Nehru gave his illustrious speech on the occasion, which started with the famous words: 'Long years ago we made a tryst with destiny, and now the time comes when we shall redeem our pledge, not wholly or in full measure, but very substantially. At the stroke of the midnight hour, when the world sleeps, India will awake to life and freedom.'

Alas neither India nor Pakistan awoke next morning to life or freedom. The administration on both sides of the border was in disarray. It was only a rumour that the new border was on the upper Bari Doab canal. The partition of India had been done in a hurried fashion without adequate planning. Despite the signs of violence and tensions between Hindus and Muslims much before Partition, only few arrangements had been made to control the obvious fallout. A refugee camp had been created in the GCUL for people who had to go to Amritsar. Riots had broken out and angry voices uttering '*La illah illa allah* (there is no God but Allah)' could be heard. Mobs carrying *mashals* (lit torches) and weapons sent shivers down the spines of non-Muslims. In Amritsar, Khalsa College was the refugee camp for the Hindus coming from Lahore.

August is a time when the monsoons recede, and not only is it hot but also extremely humid. The Lall family used to sleep out in the garden under mosquito nets, armed with whatever could be used as a weapon. One member of the family would stay awake keeping a watch on the streets where murderous mobs were running amok looting and killing. There was only a hedge between the house and the gully, which was the dominion of the mobs. Amar, giving a first-hand account of the experience, narrated how there were times when it was a huge task to get food, and the family had to manage somehow to stay alive. Amar narrated:

> I must have not slept more than three or four hours at night. The only weapons we had were the golf clubs. With these golf clubs, all the male members of the family would do two–three-hour shifts at night, walking around the house. A lot of my cousins and relatives from various parts of the city had shifted around the house and a big group of them was in our house, too. We were just lucky that nothing happened.

The Lall house was located where Jail Road, Ferozepur Road, Multan Road, Aurangzeb Road, Temple Road and Queens Road, all came together. There was a police station and a Sikh temple not far from the house. The area was called Mozang, which was largely Muslim-dominated. But there was also a fairly large Sikh population. Both communities had lived for centuries together as friends. Religion was their personal affair and never affected relationships. But all of that changed once Partition was announced. Amar's brother Chander, narrated: 'All hell broke loose.' Thousands of Hindus and Sikhs were massacred in the Mozang area. Chander described it as nothing less than a holocaust.

Amar recalled that in those days, radios were not very common and radio sets were only used by the elders. The only common source of information was the newspapers that came in every morning. However, owing to the conditions, the *Lahore Tribune* and other newspapers had stopped their publication.

Amar narrated that it was right after Partition that a Christian friend of his came over. He asked Amar to accompany him to see something he would have never seen before. They took their bicycles and rode to Mayo Hospital in Lahore, the best and most exclusive hospital in the city. About half a mile before they reached the hospital, there was an overbearing smell of decaying flesh. The smell, Amar recalled, was so overpowering that it was difficult to breathe. 'I saw the most horrible sight that I've ever seen in my life,' he said. There were hordes of bodies everywhere. He added that under usual circumstances, when someone dies, there is an autopsy, identification, police record, and so on. But now law and order had completely broken down. Mayo Hospital was a place where post-mortems were being carried out in a corner. Bodies were coming in by the hundreds. As the morgue filled up, they started lining the bodies outside the hospital without covering them, leaving them just as they came. This continued for days, and eventually the three tennis courts adjacent to the hospital also started being used for piling up bodies. As the tennis courts started to fill up, they started putting the bodies in a pile. This resulted in the creation of huge mounds of bodies.

Amar recounted the horrifying sight of the mound of bodies having reached the same height as that of the room where he was sitting and narrating the incident. He recounted that he saw, in front of him, a truckload of bodies arriving, and sweepers, with their noses covered, carrying the bodies from the dangling limbs and throwing them on the pile on a count of 'one–two–three...'

The air was rife with rumours, some of which were later found to be horrifyingly true. One such incident that Amar heard about was that a large number of Hindu women in the newly-formed Pakistan had committed suicide by jumping into a well. They had been convinced that if their husbands were killed, they would be raped. A large number of bodies were found in a well in Rawalpindi. Rioting broke out in six districts and the situation worsened each day.

Jaidev Hunna, a survivor in his 80s, remembered the night he and his Hindu family left their home and took refuge with hundreds of others in a nearby college. They thought they were safe, but that was until the arrival of the military, comprising Muslim soldiers. Jaidev said, 'We thought they had to protect us but at night they started shooting and killing all the Hindus. I was there and beside me were four or five bodies lying who had been shot and died. So I went in among the bodies and lied down, pretending that I am also dead. They came and checked the bodies and searched my pockets for money and then went away.'[2]

On the Indian Side

The situation on the Indian side of the border was no better. Budh Singh, who was SSP Amritsar, realized that a large part of the Amritsar police was Muslim. In his wisdom, Budh Singh took the decision to disarm the Muslim police. It was his way of ensuring that the police did not turn against

---

[2]Brocklehurst, Steven, 'Partition of India: "They Would Have Slaughtered Us"', *BBC News*, 12 August 2017, https://tinyurl.com/mr4yt58t. Accessed on 28 July 2023.

the Hindus in Amritsar. This was done in a very systematic manner. Arms were issued to the policemen for night patrol, and they were expected to deposit the arms back in the morning. SSP Bindra put a procedure in place that when the policemen returned their arms the next morning, the arms would be locked in a safe room and manned by policemen for protection. And the next night, arms were not issued to policemen who were Muslim. But what seemed like a wise move to handle a delicate situation added fuel to the already raging fire when the word spread that the Muslim policemen were being disarmed. This and other incidents became commonplace. Almost every act was viewed with a communal eye. The Hindus and Sikhs, being in majority in Amritsar, were able to kill and plunder Muslim residents at will.

News of the killing of the minority communities on both sides of the border fuelled more killings. The border was only 17 miles away, so those who didn't get killed, fled and crossed the border to Lahore or Amritsar. Crossing the borders, they would narrate their horror stories to their friends, families and brothers, provoking even more killing and rioting. Killings, which started a few days before Partition, picked up substantially post Partition and continued for many months.

Travel to India

While conditions in Lahore were deteriorating each day, Pushpa, Inder Mohan's youngest daughter, developed acute pain in her stomach. With some difficulty, a doctor was consulted. Dr Puri, a family friend who didn't live far from the house, came to their rescue. It was fortuitous that he had not fled to India as yet. Dr Puri diagnosed appendicitis. Pushpa had to be operated upon urgently to remove her appendix since a burst appendix could have been life-threatening. For this, she had to be taken to Sir Ganga Ram Hospital for a surgery. However, the situation did not permit them to leave the house. The journey itself could prove to be fatal not just for Pushpa but also the ones accompanying her.

As her condition deteriorated, some drastic steps had to be taken. Budh Singh was the only person who could help. He was a senior police officer at the time and could help them move to safety, but he was in Amritsar.[3] Somebody would have had to travel to Amritsar and find Budh Singh.

At a family meeting, it was decided that Budh Singh's help was needed to make arrangements for the family, or for at least Pushpa, to immediately move from Lahore to Amritsar so she could receive proper medical attention. A difficult choice had to be made for another child to undertake the risky and life-threatening journey across the border and find Budh Singh. After some deliberation, it was decided that Amar, being the eldest male member, would stay back. Chander and his cousin Krishan were asked to make the perilous journey from Lahore to Amritsar to find SSP Bindra. Amar escorted them to the DAV College Refugee Camp in Lahore, where they would spend the night and attempt to catch an early-morning lorry or bus to reach the Khalsa College Refugee Camp in Amritsar. These buses plied between the camps, transporting refugees, between what were now two countries carved out of one. The vehicles were escorted half-way, up to 27 km by Pakistan's military, from Lahore to the new border, from where the Indian Army would take over the responsibility.

---

[3]Records of the Amritsar City Police show B.S. Bindra as SSP Amritsar between 19 August 1947 and 30 September 1947.

The camp provided food and limited shelter. It was so densely packed with refugees that they had to sleep in the minimal sitting space they could find. The college buildings acted as shelters from the rain and provided lavatories. Early the next morning, they were woken up by calls from the police who were asking the refugees to board the closest transport to them. Lorries and buses were few and the number of passengers far exceeded the capacity. Chander and Krishan had to push their way on to a vehicle, before all the space was taken up. Packed beyond capacity, people clung to the sides, sat on the roof, or anywhere they could find a place to balance themselves.

The lorries and buses pulled out of the camp and travelled down Mall Road, heading south to the new border. The convoy travelled at a slow pace, followed by military vehicles to prevent mobs from jumping the buses and lorries and massacring the refugees. The vehicles drove down the railway station, and then to the Grand Trunk Road, the highway the British had built to transport people and goods from one end of India to the other, from west to east. At the border, the convoy had to stop for inspection by the military—first the Pakistan Army and then the Indian Army.

It was the month of August, which is both hot and humid, with temperatures rising above 40 degrees Celsius. Chander and Krishan saw some horrific scenes during the journey. Men, women and children compelled to abandon their homes, with great threat to their lives, had to move towards the imaginary line. Many were walking on foot, some on bullock carts, with their cows and buffaloes in tow. For the privileged, there were convoys of trucks and heavy vehicles. Others tried their luck on trains. There were people moving from India to Pakistan on one side and from Pakistan to India on the other, unaware of what lay ahead for them. Out of curiosity, they were asking questions from people coming from the other side about the conditions there. Each spoke their own dialect of Punjabi. These exchanges were fraught with risk, for they included in abundance, narratives of plunder and murder. This could ignite fresh violence amongst these tired travellers. Blame had to be attributed and, alas, it was often attributed to victims of the carnage rather than the perpetrators of it, leading to even more violence.

After two to three days of stressful travel, when the convoys coming from the Indian side would cross the border into what was now Pakistan, they would get a fresh wind in their wings. Somebody would suddenly start shouting, 'Oh we have crossed into Pakistan.' This would give a psychological boost to all those who were looking to reach Pakistan. The air would fill with chants of '*Mohammad Ali Jinnah Zindabad, Pakistan Zindabad* (Long live, Mohammad Ali Jinnah, long live Pakistan)'. The same ebullience would be felt by those crossing into India. They would chant '*Mahatma Gandhi Zindabad, Hindustan Zindabad*'. Exhausted people, after their long travel, would get a renewed burst of energy after crossing over the invisible line that separated the two countries. To vent their frustration, they would engage in stone pelting on the convoys moving in the opposite direction. This would often lead to riots and arson, and many would be killed in the process. Armies and police on both sides would attempt to provide security to the convoys, often by use of tanks, jeeps, trucks, etc. SSP Bindra later narrated to Amar how he had got a telephone call one night that a train full of butchered Hindus had reached Amritsar station. Stopping a train and butchering the travellers was a common occurrence. This train came into Amritsar with over 2,000 dead bodies. SSP

Bindra continued recounting how one man came out of the pile of bodies and fell at his feet, pleading with him that he be saved. He was covered in blood from head to toe and had to feign death throughout the entire journey. His entire family had been massacred.

Accounts of Horror

This situation was quite similar to the trains that reached Lahore. Each incident ignited and fuelled further acts of violence. An eye for an eye, tooth for a tooth. Khushwant Singh, the noted journalist, in his book *Punjab, Punjabis and Punjabiyat*, narrated his own experience:

> I read the newspaper as best as I could amidst the clucking and the quarrelling of the birds. This continued right through the spring of the year 1947. I read of the impending transfer of power from British to Indian hands, of the Boundary Commission that was to partition India and Pakistan and of the rioting that was taking place all over Punjab. I assumed that these things would pass, that India and Pakistan would be free members of the Commonwealth and that I would stay on where I was in Lahore, whether it went to India or Pakistan, and have my morning cup of tea with my white leghorn rooster and his harem of three snow maidens. The birds gave life a sense of continuity.
>
> Early in the August of 1947 things began to change. The riots assumed the magnitude of a massacre and it became clear that the Sikhs and Hindus would have to clear out of Pakistan. I was a Sikh, but I clung to the hope that I would be able to stay in Pakistan where I had

been born and where all my closest friends, who were largely Muslim, were living.

This was not to be. One afternoon in the first week of August, I saw columns of black smoke rising from the bazaars and heard sounds of gunfire and the wailing of women.

A week before Independence, Chris Everett, head of the CID in Punjab, who had studied law with me in London, advised me to get out of Lahore. We picked up whatever we could in our hands, handed the keys of the house to a Muslim friend, Manzur Qadir, and joined the stream of Hindu and Sikh refugees going out of Pakistan into India. Escorted by six Baluch constables, my wife and I took a train to Kalka to join our two children, who had been sent ahead to their grandparents in Kasauli. We came across convoys of Muslim refugees fleeing from India into Pakistan. We heard terrible stories of murder, rape and arson. I've heard that rioters who had come to loot my house in Lahore and had been beaten off by my friend had got away with my white leghorns, which happened to be in the garden. We had no doubt of the fate that had befallen them. Then I realised that the world I had lived in and whose continuance I had taken for granted had ceased to exist.

I arrived in Delhi on 13 August 1947. The next night I was amongst the crowd outside Parliament House chanting 'Bharat Mata ki Jai'. I saw Lord Louis Mountbatten lower the Union Jack as the last viceroy of British India and hoist the Indian tricolour as the first Governor-General of free India. I heard jubilant crowds singing in the streets. I saw English officers carried aloft on shoulders by enthusiastic young men—there was an

> unbelievable burst of friendship towards the English. But there was an element of unreality in the celebrations because the killing and looting went on.[4]

Author Nisid Hajari wrote in his book, *Midnight's Furies: The Deadly Legacy of India's Partition*, how gangs of murderers set entire villages on fire, hacked men and children and the aged, and also abducted young women and raped them. In his chilling narrative of the butchery, he stated,

> Some British soldiers and journalists who had witnessed the Nazi death camps, claimed partition's brutalities were worse: pregnant women had their breasts cut off and babies hacked out of their bellies, infants were found literally roasted on spits... Indeed, it does not matter which was worse. What is important to understand is that partition is to the psyche of Indians and Pakistanis what the Holocaust is to Jews.[5]

There were several other horrific stories of near misses. Seventy-six-year-old Mohindra Dhall's family lived in Lyallpur (now Faisalabad), which was on the Pakistan side of the border. Although they were Hindus, they wanted to stay there, but reports of looting and killings in the nearby villages forced them to leave. They had just a few hours to pack up and leave but when they tried to get on a train to India, it was too crowded, with people sitting on the roof and anywhere they could find the tiniest space to occupy.

'My father,' narrated Dhall, 'decided to come out of the

---

[4]Singh, Khushwant, *Punjab, Punjabis and Punjabiyat: Reflections on a Land and Its People*, Aleph Book Company, India, 2018.

[5]Hajari, Nisid, *Midnight's Furies: The Deadly Legacy of India's Partition*, Penguin Books Limited, India, 2016.

train and we stayed back, only to hear the next day that the whole train was completely butchered. Half of our friends from the village, who were on the train, got butchered.' It was his father's timely call not to board the train that ended up saving their lives.[6]

Dr Salim Ahmed, then a 22-year-old medical student, was travelling in the opposite direction in a train. As his train met with a hostile mob, he pretended to be a Christian. '"They came as a crowd," he said. "They said, 'Muslim, Muslim, Muslim', and they pulled them down from the train. They took the women and starting hitting them and started the massacre. The women were crying, 'My child, my child' but we couldn't help them. Little children, they took them and bang they killed them with a sword. They would just kill them on the ground."'[7]

Bir Raminder, Avinash and Narinder, the three of the four children of SSP Budh Singh Bindra
Source: Singh family albums

---

[6]Brocklehurst, Steven, 'Partition of India: "They Would Have Slaughtered Us"', *BBC News*, 12 August 2017, https://tinyurl.com/mr4yt58t. Accessed on 28 July 2023.
[7]Ibid.

Like the Lall family, millions of people found themselves on the 'wrong' side of the border. Ten million became refugees in what was the largest population movement in history. Muslims travelled to Pakistan; Sikhs and Hindus to India. Up to a million of these refugees were killed in a series of horrific massacres in the border regions. Some of the worst atrocities took place in Punjab. 'Despite the efforts of the 55,000-strong Punjab Boundary Force, over 200,000 people were murdered. Mountbatten was later criticized for rushing the partition process and failing to tackle the migration and communal violence that followed the birth of the new nations.'[8]

To Amritsar and Back

As Chander and Krishan completed their risk-fraught journey and reached the refugee camp in Khalsa College, Amritsar, they were and looked like refugees, wearing minimal clothing and that too torn. Thankfully, their journey had been relatively uneventful, and their convoy had not been attacked. They had survived.

Their next challenging task was to find SSP Bindra in Amritsar. All they knew was Budh Singh Bindra was a senior police officer there. This was their first trip to Amritsar, and with no money in their pockets, their only means of travel in the unfamiliar city was by foot. Chander was about 15 years at the time.

---

[8]'Independence and Partition, 1947', *National Army Museum*, https://tinyurl.com/msfnxa37. Accessed on 9 November 2023.

SSP Budh Singh Bindra and his wife Maan Kaur
Source: Singh family albums

They started with looking for a police station near Khalsa College Refugee Camp. Following directions given by locals, they reached a police station near Mall Road. Upon asking for the residence of SSP Budh Singh Bindra, they were told that it was located at the end of Mall Road. This meant many hours of walking in the sweltering heat. Being exhausted from a long journey, and with little to eat, the long walk seemed to go on for eternity. They finally reached the end of Mall Road, where they came across a bungalow with a fence around it and a heavily guarded entrance. Seeing how shabby they looked, the guards did not greet them cordially and refused to allow them entry inside the house or to even convey a message to the Bindras that two ragged looking visitors had come seeking them. After all, Budh Singh was a senior police officer and could not be bothered by some street urchins who thought they could get an audience with him.

Not knowing what to do, the two started walking around the house, and as luck would have it, through the fence they saw a house help on the other side. Speaking in Punjabi, Chander requested her to tell the *sahib* and *memsahib* that their nephew Chander Lall[9] was here to see them. Again, seeing their state, the help too could hardly believe that these could be nephews of the *sahib* and *memsahib.* Reluctantly, she agreed to go inside and convey their message.

She went indoors, and they stood outside waiting for her to return for what seemed like eternity. *Had she abandoned the idea of informing the occupants?* Chander was convinced that was the case. Thankfully, that was not to be. Maan Kaur, upon hearing Chander's name, came rushing out to see if indeed the news she had got was true. She immediately recognized Chander and instructed her staff to bring both of them inside.

Chander fondly remembers the warm embrace with which he was greeted by Maan Kaur. The Bindras had spent many sleepless nights worrying about the Lall family. This meeting was as joyous for them as it was for Chander. As they were taken inside and given some food and water, conversation veered towards the state of the Lall family in Lahore. When Maan Kaur heard about their state, and especially about Pushpa, she wept uncontrollably.

Clearly, there was no time to waste. By then it was evening, and Budh Singh had also returned from work. He was overjoyed to see the two boys. Both the children had bathed and been given fresh clothes to wear and food to eat. For the Bindra children, Chander and Krishan's visit felt like déjà vu. They were looking forward to be reunited with the Lall family.

---

[9]Not to be confused with Chander M. Lall, the author of this book, who was named after his uncle.

Budh Singh immediately instructed his subordinates to make arrangements to move the Lall family from Lahore to Amritsar. Chander, narrating this incident, said, 'Mrs Bindra was my goddess. To this day, I love her for her care and the love she shared with our family. She was a goddess who came to our rescue.'

It took two days for Budh Singh to gather resources for Chander and Krishan to return to Lahore. He arranged for a truck and a police escort to accompany them to Lahore, and get the family in the truck and return to Amritsar as fast as possible. He got all the necessary papers that would be required for the truck to travel back and forth, with all the members of the Lall family, carrying whatever household items they could carry conveniently.

Without much delay, Chander and Krishan boarded the truck and started their journey to Lahore. By the time they reached their home in Lahore, they heard the dreaded news that Pushpa had passed away a few days prior. Her appendix had burst and she could not receive timely medical attention. In fact, she could not receive any medical attention whatsoever. Chander narrated with a heavy heart, 'Pushpa had died of a burst appendix and had to be cremated. All this happened in the four or so days that were spent crossing the border, finding the Bindra family and arranging to get transportation to rescue the family. I was devastated at Pushpa's passing away at this critical time. Had we arrived a day or so earlier, we could have possibly saved her. The only thing we could do was get all the remaining family members in the truck and head for the border...'

The grief was insurmountable. The youngest girl child always has a special place in everybody's heart. Jogi, the youngest son of Inder Mohan, reminiscing about his sister

Pushpa, said that he was completely shattered by her death. Even years after her death, seeing a picture of hers brought tears to his eyes. 'Pushpa and I were very close, and after her death, I did not want to live anymore,' Jogi said. He was not in Lahore when Pushpa passed away and was not told of her death for a long time. When the news was eventually broken to him, it left him shell-shocked. 'I used to sit on a tree for hours thinking of where Pushpa had gone… I longed to see her even if it was just once. How could she just disappear without even saying bye to me?' lamented Jogi.

It was under this backdrop that the tormented Lall family had to undertake the task of cremating Pushpa. Sorrow and melancholy had to be put aside and wise decisions had to be taken regarding her cremation. However, taking her mortal remains to a crematorium would be a clear giveaway that they were Hindus. The chances of surviving the mobs in such a situation would be virtually nil.

Since Inder Mohan had been a sessions judge in the area, Amar used his connections to reach out to the magistrate in Lahore. Arrangements were made to take the body to the crematorium in the magistrate's car, accompanied by police escorts.

Despite the dangers, Dropadi insisted on staying a few more days in Lahore, to perform the last rites of her daughter. Her ashes had to be collected and immersed and ceremonies performed for her soul to find a place in heaven, at the feet of the Lord. Hindus cremate their dead as they believe that a body is merely a vehicle for the soul, and once the soul leaves the body, the vehicle becomes irrelevant. Cremation is considered the quickest way to release the soul and help in its reincarnation.

Leaving for India

Having completed the last rites of Pushpa, Amar now had the unenviable task of shifting the family base out of Lahore. Amar was 19 years, Savitri was 18, Sheila was 17, Chander was 15, Billy was 13 and Jogi was merely 8. There was also Amar's grandmother Amma, who had been moved from Mianwali to Lahore.

While Pushpa's last rites were performed over a period of a few days, Amar started to work with the authorities to move his family to Amritsar. Budh Singh had made all the arrangements for a truck that would carry the family. This truck would depart from the DAV College, an institution run and managed by a Hindu religious trust, and it was being made into a camp where Hindus could assemble and then be taken to Amritsar. Owing to the situation in Lahore, which was now a part of Pakistan, the camp was run by Hindus and protected by the Indian Army.

As per the arrangements, the trucks were leaving from the DAV College, so Amar had to make a few trips from home to the DAV College on a bicycle. He had to ensure that it was safe for the family to eventually make this journey and board the truck. During these trips, Amar ensured he was not dressed in a manner that would give away his identify as a Hindu. On the way, he would often cross large crowds shouting '*Mohammad Ali Jinnah Zindabad, Pakistan Zindabad*'. One day, a large crowd was gathered around a man lying in the middle of the road in a pool of blood. There was nothing that Amar or anybody could have done to save this man. Being a Hindu himself, Amar did not think it wise to stop and inquire and instead cycled away from the scene quickly.

Upon reaching the DAV College one day, Amar found

that a social worker was in-charge of the camp. As he tried to reach out to her to seek help, a man came running and informed everybody how a Christian man had been stabbed to death. He was a senior official at the Punjab University and had taken the gruelling journey to India from Lahore. He was returning to Lahore to hand over the charge to his successor. He probably thought that since he was Christian, he would not be in any danger, but tragically, he was stabbed to death by a subordinate he had dismissed a few months earlier. Under the guise of communal violence, the university official had been killed. His conscientiousness towards the university cost him his life.

This was not the only encounter Amar experienced. A neighbour who lived a quarter of a mile away from their Lahore home decided to return to Lahore to collect some cash that he had hidden in his house. The local mobs got information about him, and he was held, stabbed and grievously injured. Somehow, he drove himself to Sir Ganga Ram Hospital, but succumbed to his injuries just outside it.

The DAV College was teeming with people scrambling on to any vehicle that was leaving, and the chances of him getting his whole family to Amritsar through this route seemed bleak. Arrangements were, therefore, made for the truck to pick them up from their home.

They had one truck in which they could carry themselves and whatever household belongings they had. Inder Mohan had a collection of Gandhara statues, which he had picked up from abandoned temples in what is now Pakistan. He had also commissioned the making of a dining table in pure teak wood. This dining table was accompanied by 12 chairs, also made of teak. The insignia on the back of the chairs had been chosen to be the Lion Capital of Ashoka emblem. These chairs had been commissioned well before Partition. Later, the Lion Capital of Ashoka became the national emblem of India. The dining table and chairs were thus left in the house itself.

As far as the Gandhara statues were concerned, Amar requested one of his Muslim friends to hide them in his house. Amar assured the friend that he would return for the statues. Judging by the situation in Lahore, the retention of Hindu statues in a Muslim house would hardly be considered wise. Accordingly, it was decided that the statues would be buried in the backyard of the house. The family also had a revolver in their possession. Amar personally undertook this task. He made a deep hole in the backyard and hid the statues and the gun. The family also had a Studebaker car, which was their prized possession in Lahore. The car was parked and left at the house of the secretary to the governor for safekeeping by one of Amar's friends. Only the bare necessities were packed, including some basic bedding and a few woollens. All these things came in handy after they reached Amritsar.

Upon reaching Amritsar, the Lall family was greeted with open arms by the Bindras. The children of the two families were delighted to be reunited. For them, living under one roof together felt like an adventure.

Once the family was safe in Amritsar, the fear and uncertainty of the previous weeks seemed to vanish. The border was still porous and Amar took a number of trips over the succeeding months. Since he wore the mantle of being the eldest male member of the family at the time, he took it upon himself to salvage as many of the household articles as he probably could. At other times, he simply went to meet his friends.

Hindus and Muslims had always lived as neighbours and in peace. 'Our forefathers,' Amar said in retrospect, 'had lived through Muslims invasions of India. Mahmud of Ghazni came here 17 times as a glorified robber. He came here 17 times with the sole intention to loot. He went as far as Gujarat, where he even plundered the famous temple of Somnath, which had gold doors. He even dismantled those doors and carried them away. My forefathers lived through that entire period. There was never a thought that we would have to leave. We had become a part of that territory and there was no question why we would have to leave. If it became Pakistan, it became Pakistan, so what?'[10]

Author William Dalrymple called this a terrible outbreak of sectarian violence—Hindus and Sikhs on one side and Muslims on the other—'a mutual genocide' that was 'as unexpected as it was unprecedented'.[11]

Some Light in the Darkness

Amidst all the killing and pillage, there were also stories of hope and friendship that Amar narrated. One concerned his maternal uncle, Sunder Das. When Inder Mohan left for England in April 1947, he requested Sunder Das to come and stay with the family in Lahore. Sunder Das[12] was a retired police officer and was suffering from arthritis. He had earlier been staying in Mianwali. At the time of Partition, one local Pathan from Mianwali, a friend of Sunder Das, came to visit

[10]As narrated by Amar to Julie Winoeker, a journalist from San Francisco, who travelled to India and extensively interviewed Amar. The author has the original recordings in his possession.

[11]Dalrymple, William, 'The Great Divide', *The New Yorker*, 22 June 2015, https://tinyurl.com/2p8v76kn. Accessed on 3 November 2023.

[12]This is the same Sunder Das whose recruitment formed the trigger for the dismissal of I.M. Lall. He later joined the police.

their house in Lahore. Pathans are Muslims and the Lall family had many friends among them, having lived peacefully together for generations. Upon learning that the Lall family was going to leave for India, he reached out to Amma (Amar's paternal grandmother) who was still in Mianwali, and following the Hindu custom, he touched her feet and said, 'Look mother, I am sorry that you have to leave but I am totally helpless in this matter. Please forgive us.' Amma blessed him and asked him for a favour. She handed him a steel box, saying it carried all her worldly possessions. She said she was too old to carry the box with her and requested him to keep it in safe custody with himself. After handing over the box to the Pathan, Amma was escorted to Lahore by Amar, and then finally, after Partition, to Amritsar.

Amma was always keen to recover the steel box, and an opportunity came many months later when two of her nephews said that they would be travelling to Mianwali from India. Amma asked them to meet the Pathan and ask for the steel box. The two nephews had a cousin in Mianwali, who despite being Hindu, had decided to stay back in Pakistan. The cousin was very friendly with some Muslims and used to look after their wine business. When the two nephews reached Mianwali, they proceeded to the wine shop where the cousin was working. Mianwali, at the time, was a small town with a population of no more than 10,000 people. The word got around and people started pouring in to meet them. Everybody was keen on hearing stories about India. The Pathan who had taken the steel box for safe keeping also met them. He had been engaged in litigation in the district court and when he heard that these two gentlemen had come from India looking for him, he caught a tonga and met the two brothers. When they asked for the box, the Pathan told them, 'Look, we have everything that you asked us to save for you, but right now we are involved in this litigation. However, if you come back in the evening, we will hand over the box to you.' As promised, in the evening, he brought the box. At the Pathan's insistence, the box was opened and everything Amma had told them about was found intact.

In all the communal strife, Mianwali was an oasis, with hardly any killing and minimal desecration having taken place. It could be compared to the NWFP region of Pakistan, where the situation was similar. The fewer killings in these places were on account of the positive political influence in these areas. The NWFP was largely under the influence of Abdul Ghaffar Khan, also known as Bacha Khan and by some as Sarhadi Gandhi or Frontier Gandhi owing to his Gandhian approach to non-violence and his opposition to Partition. He had started the Khudai Khidmatgar or the Red Shirt Movement. It was his influence in the region that had saved many Hindu lives. Though the Hindu population in the region was no more than 10 per cent, Bacha Khan made sure that every Hindu house was under protection. Amar narrated how Hindus lived in areas where there was a concentration of Hindus, for they were a minority otherwise. Bacha Khan ensured that his Red Shirt volunteers protected the Hindu communities. He also ensured that those who wanted to leave were put on a train, guarded by the Pakistani and Indian army.

In Mianwali, according to Amar, just when the killings started, they immediately collected all the Hindus—few in number—and put them in a camp. As soon as trains were available, they were sent to Amritsar. Amar, who shuttled extensively between Amritsar and Lahore, saw one of the trains that came from Mianwali into Amritsar. He recounted how they expatiated about killings not taking place in Mianwali at all, but there were incidents of killings on the way. Amar's maternal grandmother had been on one such train. She was over 90 years at the time, and had undertaken this journey over three days and three nights without any food or water. Trains were often delayed owing to skirmishes on the way. Survival during these journeys sometimes meant chewing on raw ears of wheat, which they carried in small sacks. Once these trains would reach Amritsar, all occupants would be taken to refugee camps.

Amar's Adventures

Amar had taken it upon himself to locate as many family members as possible. In Amritsar, he would spend his time searching for family members in the refugee camps at DAV College and Khalsa College. According to Amar's narration, he met with over 200 relatives, from his mother's as well as his father's sides of the family. These included his father's two sisters. One of the sisters was already married, so her entire family was with her. There were other uncles and aunts, cousins and other immediate and distant relatives.

He also met his maternal grandmother. He recounted how the poor lady, over 90, had gone through so much. When he greeted her with, 'Grandmother I have come to take you', she broke down and said, 'Son, I cannot walk or stand.' She was extremely feeble and weak. Amar arranged for a cycle rickshaw to take her out of the refugee camp. Though she survived this ordeal, she passed away soon thereafter. Amma, Amar's paternal grandmother, lived for a long time. According to him, she must have been around 100 when she eventually died. In those days, nobody kept track of their age.

One of the attractions that motivated Amar to return to Pakistan, despite the dangers of the journey, was his gang of four friends, Prem, Amar, Liakat and Sadiq, who had christened their assemblage as PALS. Liakat who Sadiq stayed back in Pakistan, whilst Prem settled in Varanasi, Uttar Pradesh, in India. Zia, though born in Lyallpur, spent his initial days in Lahore, and was very much a part of PALS.

During one of his retrospections, Liakat quipped about Amar's daring trips to Lahore, being taken to a police station with Zia, being rescued by Zia's cousin, getting his car back, riding to Dilli Darwaza on a cycle, with Liakat threatening to call aloud his Hindu name near burning houses, in jest and to put the fear of God in him. Amar would threaten to kill Liakat before he could do so. This narrative gives an insight into how despite the seriousness of the situation, the friends found moments to indulge in banter.

However, not all of Amar's trips back and forth between Lahore and Amritsar were free of danger. It was early September 1974, when Liakat was in Lyallpur, having just returned from Kashmir. Amar had returned to Lahore in his efforts to retrieve whatever he could from their house. On this trip, the agenda was to take back to India the Studebaker car lying in their house. The plan was to stack the car with Kraft cheese. Amar's paternal uncle, Chiman Ahuja, first cousin of Inder Mohan, had purchased the Kraft cheese from a customs auction with the hope of selling it in retail and profiting from it, but Partition had brought his plans to a halt. Amar would often sell the cheese in small quantities to fund his trips to Lahore. He would also use the money to partake in celebrations with his friends at the Lorang Tea House in Lahore. At 19, life itself was a celebration for him despite the odds. Zia recalled that, during Amar's visits, he had so much Kraft cheese that he never wanted to have it again in life.

It was time for Amar to return to Amritsar with the car. Zia and Amar proceeded to the Lall house and stacked the car with cans of Kraft cheese. The plan was for Amar to drop Zia at his house and proceed to drive to Lahore via the Wagah Border. By now, word had got around that a Hindu had returned to Pakistan and was trying to take goods out of his house. The police reached the spot and arrested both Amar and Zia, and took them to the police station, along with the car. These were tense moments because the administration had completely broken down, and the police held supreme powers. As Zia and Amar entered the police station, on one side of the entrance were six bodies of—judging by the length of their hair—Sikhs. Many had bullet wounds in their chests. 'It was the most horrifying sight I have ever seen,' Zia narrated. At the time I interviewed Zia, he was almost 90. The memory made him quiver, even that day.

The situation was extremely tense, with lives of both Amar and Zia in danger. At the time in Pakistan, Hindus were a disposable commodity and an accompanying Muslim could be equally vulnerable. Mass killings were taking place and another missing Hindu would hardly be noticed. Clearly, the police were more interested in the Studebaker car. Both Amar and Zia were interrogated by the police with respect to their identities and what they were doing with the car. When asked, Amar initially gave his name as Anwar, but when the sub-inspector raised his voice and asked for his full name, out of sheer fear, Amar had to reveal his real name and his identity as a Hindu.

Amar's life was clearly on the line and Zia, perhaps, was the only stumbling block between the police and the car. Killing them both and adding them to the six bodies

Amar Lall
Source: Lall family albums

was an obvious option for the police, and according to Amar, the possibility was very real.

While Amar realized how precarious his position was, Zia knew that the police were only interested in the car. He took the sub-inspector into a separate room and told him that though Amar was a Hindu, he was a friend, and he was not going to abandon him there in the police station. As a quid pro quo, he said that the police could keep the car so long as they let go of both of them. The deal was struck, and both of them were released and asked to leave quietly.

There was now another problem. As the information about a Hindu being in Lahore spread, an enraged crowd gathered outside the police station. The police had simply let them leave the police station but could not provide them with protection from the mob. That was a problem that Zia and Amar would have to deal with themselves. Zia realized that he could help Amar only if he could find a safe way out of the police station. Zia, who eventually went on to become a famous Pakistani actor, put on his best histrionics. As he stepped out of the police station, he started shouting at Amar as if he was not a friend and only an acquaintance. In his repartee, Zia screamed at Amar calling him a *kafir* and blamed him for getting them in this position. He categorically told Amar that he was not going to risk his life for him, a Hindu, and that he was inclined to leave Amar to his fate. Amar did not catch on to Zia's stagecraft, and broke into a sweat, pleading with Zia to not leave him at the mercy of the murderous mob. According to Amar's narrative, he had never seen death so close. He begged Zia not to abandon him, but the latter did not relent.

Madan, Sadiq and Amar in Lahore
Source: Liakat Hayat Khan

Deceived by Zia's conduct, the mob allowed him to leave and Amar was compelled to stay in the police station. As Zia left the police station, Amar realized that he was in extremis, as he could overhear conversations of the police in Urdu, about how the mob would kill Amar if he tried to leave. He was not safe in the police station either.

As Zia stepped out of the police station, he started running helter-skelter to look for help for Amar. He knew he had very little time. Fortuitously, he met his friend Ilyas, who was alone on a motorcycle. Zia stopped Ilyas and told him that time was short and asked him to drive into the police station and get Amar out. Ilyas was warned that this operation had to be quick and efficient.

Without further ado, Ilyas drove full speed into the police station. As he drove in, he saw Amar sitting on a bench close to the entrance. Two policemen were at a distance from Amar.

As Ilyas approached Amar, he shouted to Amar to jump on his bike. Amar, who was sitting on the edge of the bench, reacted quickly and jumped onto the backseat of Ilyas' motorcycle. Before the police or the mob could react, they had driven away. They met Zia outside and he too jumped on to the motorcycle. The mob started to chase them, but their feet were no match for the speed of the motorcycle.

They headed for Zia's house, which seemed the safest place at present for the three of them. Within the precincts of safe harbour, as their heartbeats, adrenaline and cortisol levels returned to normal, they all chortled in delight. When Ilyas was told the entire story, his initial joy and excitement were replaced with perturbation and anxiety, but now that the dangers were behind them, he felt proud to have been part of this memorable triumph.

Amar Lall
Source: Lall family albums

Amar could not have stayed at Zia's house, as it was already overcrowded with many Muslim refugees from India, and harbouring a Hindu in the house may not have been appropriate. Amar had a friend Arthur, whose father was a priest in the Lahore cathedral, so a decision was taken that the three of them would ride on the motorcycle to the cathedral. As they started to ride, they could see a mob at a distance, which recognized the motorcycle and its three riders. The chase started once again. The motorcycle and the pillion riders were now too conspicuous, and if the mob saw the motorcycle going to the cathedral, their actions could put the cathedral in danger. A quick decision was made: as they would turn round the corner, Amar would jump off the running motorcycle and hide, and then stealthily find his way to the cathedral. He could perhaps even merge with the mob at some point.

As they turned the corner, away from the glare of the mob, Amar jumped and hid under a bridge. His heart was pounding as the unruly and recalcitrant mob passed him by. Thankfully, they had not noticed Amar and proceeded to chase the motorcycle. Amar stealthily found his way to the cathedral where he spent the next three nights. There, too, he had to stay hidden in the attic, as Arthur's father would not have permitted Amar to stay and risk the cathedral.

Once the immediate danger to Amar's life had subsided, the friends again met at Zia's house where the entire incident was then narrated to Zia's father, and his help was sought in the release of the car. Studebaker cars were a rare commodity at the time, and this one, a Studebaker Commander, had been specially imported from England by Inder Mohan. Amar would not let the police take away the car. He had to get it back to India.

The issue was how to get the car out of the police station.

Zia's father, Khadim Mohyeddin, was a mathematician, musicologist, playwright and lyricist, also associated with various theatre groups, and hence fairly influential in Lahore. He called the police station. Speaking in a commanding voice, he directed the police to release the car on the pretext that he was calling from the governor's house. Upon receiving his call, the policemen, panic-stricken, represented to him that they never had any intentions of harming any of the boys and that they would happily return the car. Amar was then asked to go back to the police station and get his car, but he was having none of it. So, Zia was sent with an escort to go and get the car, and finally the car was released.

In the meantime, one of Amar's cousins, who was also in Lahore, learnt that Amar had been taken to the police station. He had no further information thereafter. The cousin found his way to Amritsar and visited the family who were with the Bindras and informed them about Amar's condition. According to him, Amar had perhaps been killed. Amar's younger brother, Chander, was immediately sent to Lahore in an armoured vehicle with two police personnel to go locate Amar. With some difficulty, they were able to locate Amar, and he was taken back to Amritsar in the armoured vehicle.

Amar would return to Lahore in a few months' time, in another effort to get the Studebaker car back, which was parked and left at the house of the secretary to the governor. Once again, Amar reached out to Zia's father and requested Zia to accompany him to the secretary's house, perhaps to put added pressure to hand over the car to them. Partition was such an event that those who held properties in trust expected the properties to be with them forever, virtually as owners. Amar's trip to the secretary's house completely took them by surprise. Their reluctance to hand back the car was palpable.

However, as a measure of respect for Inder Mohan and Zia, the secretary to the governor handed over the car to Amar.

The car became an object of extreme joy for Amar and the *chandaal chokri*[13]. The cheese and the car made an ideal combination, one providing the money and the other, transport. As soon as the car was recovered, Amar and the boys decided to go for a spin. The problem was that petrol was in short supply in those days. A decision was made to steal petrol from the flying club, and off they went, sneaking into the flying club to get fuel. Once the car had its fill, Falletti's, a well-known Lahore hotel, restaurant and bakery, became the next destination.

Left to right: Prem, Amar, Liakat and Sadiq; Col. Brown's School, Dehradun, 1942
Source: Liakat Hayat Khan

Eventually, Amar decided to drive the car back to India. In addition to the rest of the cheese, he also decided to carry the

[13]An expression used to describe a boisterous group.

Gandhara statues back with him. To retrieve the statues, he visited the house of his friend where they were buried. He had already contacted the friend and asked him to dig the statues out of the ground, which he had done. To Amar's dismay, one of the statues had been damaged, with the face of the deity having been mutilated. The friend said that he had mistakenly damaged the statue while digging it out. These were Gandhara statues of around the fifth century. The remaining statues were stacked in the Studebaker Commander car, and cheese was stacked on the top to hide them. Amar hoped to cross the border without being enquired.

Needless to say, he was stopped at the border and the policeman at the border asked for papers permitting the car and other materials to be taken out of Pakistan. Amar was asked to step out of the car and invited inside the police station. This time, Zia was not around to rescue him and memories of the recent escape flooded his mind. He could not afford to break into a sweat or show any signs of fear or discomposure. The histrionics would have to be his own. He would have to sound influential and armed with all the necessary paperwork and ensure that the policemen did not search his car. If the statues were discovered, his chances of getting away would be very distant.

Putting up a brave face, Amar asked, 'What kind of papers do you want to see?' The head constable said that he wanted to see the permit for the car to be taken out of Pakistan. Amar had no idea that a permit was required and needless to say, he did not have one. He knew he would have to maintain a poker face and be completely inscrutable. A mismatch between the brain, which was in a confused and distressed state, and the face, which had to give an impression of confidence, could cost him his life.

Amar realized that in his pocket was a piece of paper given to him by the Custodian of Evacuee Properties at that time. Of course, this paper was dated, and had items that Amar had already removed from the house. Thinking on his feet, Amar hazarded a guess that the policeman, being a head constable, which was a low rank, would not understand or read English and would therefore not be able to read the paper that he pulled out of his pocket. Amar felt the document looked reasonably official, and he showed it to the policeman with complete confidence, introducing it as the permit for the car and what was contained therein. The poor constable could only try and look intelligent while inspecting the same. 'I could see from the look on his face that he couldn't read a word from it,' narrated Amar. The head constable gave Amar a green signal after taking down the car number and its model and make. He was also made to sign a register.

As he got into the car again and started the car, it stalled—there was some trouble with the battery. He then had the audacity to go back to the head constable. Massaging the latter's ego, he referred to him as inspector *sahib* and said, 'Inspector Sahib, you stopped me and now my car won't start, can you help me push it.' So, the head constable, along with two other constables, pushed Amar's car to help get it started. Amar, with a wry smile, reminisced how the poor fellows were made to push start the car, so he could head to the border.

This was just one of the numerous trips that he made back to Lahore. Liakat was in Lyallpur at the time but would come to Lahore often to meet Amar. Amar had an innate sense of fearlessness and adventure, and his friends did not find it amiss that despite such bloodshed, Amar was travelling across the border frequently. Kraft cheese was his currency of choice, as it could be converted to paper currency with ease, giving sufficient resources for him and his friends to enjoy a meal at Faletti's.

On yet another trip, SSP Bindra was able to provide Amar with a truck to carry back the household materials from the Lahore house. Amar picked the dining table and chairs, which now find a place of pride in Amar's home in Delhi, along with the Gandhara statues. Whilst Amar continued to make trips back and forth, eventually the abandoned house was taken over, and he could no longer visit or stay there. He then started to spend the nights with his friends, and at other times, at a cathedral, where he knew the chaplain, who would let him sleep there. One evening, however, Amar overheard the chaplain's family discussing how dangerous it was for them to shelter him. He left quietly and never returned, as he did not want to endanger the chaplain or his family. This also put an end to his trips to Lahore, for the time being, though he would continue to have a deep connection with the city and his friends.

Left to right: Madan, Sadiq, Mukhtar, Amar and Liakat at the Lahore canal
Source: Liakat Hayat Khan

9

Appeal to the Privy Council (1947)

While the family was undergoing the turmoil of Partition, and Amar was having his own adventures, Inder Mohan was defending his case before the Privy Council.[1] The appeal in the Privy Council was heard by a Bench of Lord William Watson, Baron Thankerton, Herbert du Parcq, Baron du Parq, Geoffrey Lawrence, 1st Baron Oaksey, Fergus Morton, Baron Morton of Henryton and M.R. Jayakar.

The appeal against the Federal Court order was sought before the Privy Council by the Secretary of State for India. Post Partition, since the post of Secretary of State for India was abolished, the appeal was continued by the High Commissioner for India. Inder Mohan reached London in April 1947 and the hearing in the case commenced in late July 1947. As Britain was preparing for a transfer of power, the Government of India decided to excuse itself from the appeal. A letter, dated 8 August 1946, from the office of the Secretary of State to the Punjab government informed the latter of its decision of withdrawal:

[1]The Privy Council was a judicial body, which heard appeals from various courts of the British colonies, including India. Following the replacement of the Federal Court with the Supreme Court of India in January 1950, the Abolition of Privy Council Jurisdiction Act 1949 came into effect, ending the right of appeal to the Judicial Committee of the Privy Council.

> Regarding the incidence or the costs in connection with this suit. So far as those already incurred are concerned the Secretary of State would prefer to await the result of the appeal before making a direction in the matter under section 179(1) of the Government of India Act. He has, however, directed, in view of the Government of India's decision not to proceed further with the case so far as they are concerned, that the future costs of the appeal shall be paid out of the revenues of the Government of the Punjab… appellant must pay the costs of the Respondent in the appeal as between solicitor and client in any event and that the future costs of the Respondent will accordingly be included in the costs that it will fall to the Government of the Punjab to meet under this direction.[2]

So confident was Inder Mohan of success in the appeal that he agreed to the conditions of bearing the costs should he lose.

The initial period in London was spent by Inder Mohan to study the case in detail and also appointing and briefing his counsel. Sir David Maxwell Fyfe, King's Counsel (KC), and T.B.W. Ramsay, barrister-at-law, were appointed to represent Inder Mohan. Sir Fyfe was not just a politician but also a lawyer and a judge who had combined an industrious and precocious legal career with political ambitions that took him to the offices of the Solicitor General, Attorney General, Home Secretary and Lord High Chancellor of Great Britain. He was one of the prosecutors at the Nuremberg trials and was instrumental in drafting the European Convention on Human Rights. He was given the title of Earl of Kilmuir, a title which he enjoyed between 1954 and 1962.

---

[2]Author possesses a copy of the said document in his personal archives.

To

King-Emperor's Most Excellent Majesty.

The humble memorial of Mr. Indra Mohan Lall
of the Indian Civil Service.

May it please Your Majesty,

1. I hereby bring to Your Majesty's notice a case of gross injustice in the hope that Your Majesty as the ultimate fountain-head of justice will be able to redress it.

2. I was until June 1940 in Your Majesty's Civil Service in India. The Chief Secretary Punjab Government informed me in his letter No.1342-S.G-40/4773-S that as a result of the inquiry held into my conduct "the Secretary of State for India has ordered" my removal from the Indian Civil Service.

3. I have no right of appeal against this illegal and improper order.

4. Books on administrative law say that Your Majesty is "the fountain of justice" and that individuals have " the right to present a petition for justice". This petition is presented in the exercise of that right.

5. It is recorded in my covenant which the Secretary of State has broken that my service was "to continue during the pleasure of His Majesty, His Heirs and Successors to be signified under the hand of the Secretary of State for India". This covenant was under the old Government of India Act and is in correct legal form.

6. Under the new Government of India Act ([illegible] ived.

Opening page of I.M. Lall's appeal to the Privy Council
Source: The British Library

Copy of a letter No.76[illegible]96/45-Ests, dated the the 26th October, 1945, from the Government of India, Home Department, to the Chief Secretary to the Government of the Punjab.

Subject:- Suit No.42 of 1943(Federal Court Appeal No.XII of 1944)- I.M. Lall versus the Secretary of State.

As the Provincial Government are aware, an appeal against the decision of the Federal Court in the above-mentioned case is now pending before the Privy Council. The main reason why this appeal has been preferred by the Secretary of State is that the following two important points are involved in the case:-

(i) Interpretation of section 240(3) of the Government of India Act, 1935, in the matter of "a reasonable opportunity of showing cause against the action proposed to be taken".

(ii) Liability of the Crown, or the Secretary of State, for damages for wrongful dismissal in view of the fact that every member of a civil service of the Crown in India, or every person who holds a civil post under the Crown in India, holds office during His Majesty's pleasure.

2. A suggestion has now been made that in the altered circumstances the Secretary of State should be moved to withdraw the appeal in question. The Government of India have considered the suggestion, and it appears to them that it should be examined from two aspects, viz.,

(a) Mr. Lall's own personal interest, and

(b) the general public interest in seeking an authoritative interpretation of the relevant provisions of the Government of India Act, 1935.

3. As regards (a), the finding of the Federal Court is that the enquiry conducted on behalf of the Punjab Government against Mr. Lall has not prejudiced him in his defence of the charges. It does not appear that it would be proper at this stage to re-open Mr. Lall's case on merits. The financial stake involved

Correspondence between the Home Department and the Chief Secretary, Government of Punjab, suggesting withdrawal from the case

Source: National Archives of India

4. I am also to a.d that the question of interpretation of section 240(3) of the Government of India Act, 1935, referred to vide item (i) of paragraph 1 of the letter under reply is likely to recur under any constitution.

Communication from the office of the Secretary of State for India, acknowledging the wider implications of the case
Source: National Archives of India

Opposing Inder Mohan on behalf of the Crown was Sir Andrew Clark, KC. Clark was called to the Bar by the Inner Temple in 1928 and joined Lincoln's Inn in 1930. After pupillage with Raymond Evershed, who later went on to become Lord Evershed, Master of the Rolls, at the Privy Council, Clark joined the Chancery Bar and built a successful practice. In 1939, he was recalled to military service and served in a number of senior administrative posts. He reached the rank of lieutenant-colonel and honorary brigadier, and was appointed Most Excellence Order of the British Empire (Military Division). Clark became a KC in 1943 and was elected Bencher of the Inner Temple in 1951. The opposing counsel also included B. MacKenna.

Argument and Counter-Argument

The decision of the Privy Council recorded that arguments of the case commenced on 23 July 1947 and ended on 30 July 1947. In between, hearings were held on 23, 24, 28 and 29 July. The principal argument of the Crown as presented by Andrew Clark and B. MacKenna was on two counts: the first being that a civil servant is appointed at the pleasure of the King and not as a result of a contract, and the second that the 'King can do no wrong'. Resultantly, the Crown argued that Inder Mohan neither had a case in breach of contract nor under tort law.[3] The only remedy that Inder Mohan had, the Crown argued, was through administrative channels by making an appeal to the Secretary of State.

On the matter of whether Inder Mohan was given sufficient opportunity to defend his position, the Crown argued that under the prevailing laws, the Governor General had the right to cancel a commission even without providing the officer, whose commission is being cancelled, a reasonable opportunity to show cause. They argued that though Inder Mohan was given sufficient opportunity, he could be dismissed from service even if he had not been given such an opportunity, and that his dismissal was still effective. There can be no restrictions on the right of His Majesty to terminate employment at his pleasure.

Inder Mohan's response in a nutshell, as set out in the petition to the Privy Council, was:

> As far as is known Your Majesty has not directed that the power of removal or dismissal should be exercised on your behalf by the Secretary of State for India. The exercise of such power by him in my humble submission, is without authority, arbitrary and illegal. His order removing me from the Civil Service is consequently of no legal validity whatsoever.[4]

In response, as recorded in the decision, Sir Fyfe, presenting arguments on behalf of Inder Mohan, submitted that the

---

[3]A tort is an act or omission by a person giving rise to injury or harm to another and amounts to a civil wrong for which courts impose liability.

[4]Author possesses a copy of the said document in his personal archives.

terms of service of a civil servant warrant an inquiry before his services are dismissed, and if the Crown breaks the term of service, then it is answerable in damages. The introduction in the terms of service containing the qualification 'on the pleasure' does not imply otherwise. It was argued that Inder Mohan undoubtedly had an opportunity to make representations to the Federal Public Service Commission through Anderson. However, that opportunity could not be termed a reasonable opportunity if he did not know what the findings were. Additionally, Sir Fyfe argued that the opportunity to address punishment on matters where he was found guilty is an important right and there is no answer to speculate as to its value. He concluded that Inder Mohan did not get sufficient opportunity to defend his case and that the inquiry was not in accordance with natural justice.

Challenging the constitutional validity of Rule 55 of the Civil Services (Classification, Control and Appeal) Rules, Inder Mohan elucidated in his petition:

> My submission is that Rule 55 is no longer in force and that under it the inquiry could not be ordered by the Punjab Government... Classification rules were made under section 96. B(2) of the Government of India Act (5 & 6 Geo. 5 Ch 61, 6 & 7 Geo 5 Ch 37, and 9 & 10 Geo 5 Ch 101). This Act was repealed by the New Government of India Act (26 Geo. 5. Ch. 2). This Act came into force in April 1936. Presumably after the date, the Classification Rules would be considered repealed unless they are saved from repeal by the Interpretation Act or by any provision contained in the new Act.[5]

[5]Author possesses a copy of the said document in his personal archives.

In the succeeding arguments, Inder Mohan also pointed out various anomalies and puzzling conclusions in the report submitted by Brayne. In his petition, it was stated how Brayne himself pointed out the unreliability of the clerk of the court, Chaman Lall:

> He refers to my statement that these petitions 'do not appear to have been placed before me' and that 'my eyes did not see these petitions' and remarks 'I can find no direct evidence (eloquent admission of the truth of my statement) that these petitions were actually put before him except for the statement of the clerk of court... I would rather not trust the clerk of court, however, both on account of his alleged relations with Mr. Lall and his admitted unreliability.' I am grateful to Mr. Brayne for his very expressive finding about Chaman Lall. This remark is in the middle of page 17.
>
> And yet, according to this finding, I did not transgress 'the letter of it' but 'transgressed the spirit of it'. After all the mental exercise that Mr. Brayne performed while discussing this simple matter he reached such an absurd and contradictory conclusion and this is because he would not accept the obvious and the reasonable. On charge No. 2 he found, 'that there is no proof that the breach of the circular was conscious and deliberate'. On charge No. 5 the finding was that I knew the circular order and 'transgressed the spirit of it', (it is found that I did so deliberately), but I did not deliberately transgress the letter of it'. Mr. Brayne had not explained how a person who does not deliberately transgress the letter of the circular can still deliberately transgress the spirit of it.

> [...] Further on in his report Mr Brayne remarks, 'the very defects of the note create a strong suspicion that it was done to please not to catch Mr. Lall. I have been condemned on a 'strong suspicion'. Suspicion according to Mr. Brayne is as good as proof. And Mr. Brayne does not find that the note was written at 'my bidding'. It was written to 'please Mr. Lall' but without his knowledge. Again Mr. Brayne writes 'If the clerk of court was favouring Sunder Dass, he would certainly never allow Mr. Lall to be unaware of any assistance given to Sunder Dass. Mr. Lall must have known what was happening.' This is all conjecture. Mr. Lall must have known. Where is the evidence that Mr Lall in fact knew?[6]

'In my case,' he added, 'Mr Brayne has been guilty of what the lawyers call *suppressio veri* and *suggestio falsi*.' In such a situation, the injured party can seek relief from the court.

In its rejoinder arguments, the Crown argued by reiterating that just as no claim could lie against the East India Company, similarly, no claim could lie against His Majesty. They argued that Inder Mohan, the servant of the Crown, knew the charges against him and had been given a reasonable chance of defending himself against them.

By the time arguments were concluded on 30 July 1947, India was already on the brink of Partition. Resultantly, the powers of the Secretary of State abated, and so did its appeal. The appeal was, however, continued by the high commissioners of the newly formed countries, i.e., India and Pakistan.

Inder Mohan continued to live in London awaiting the decision of the Privy Council. He could now finally contact

---

[6]Author possesses a copy of the said document in his personal archives.

his family in India and hear the calamitous news of the state of his family during Partition and the death of his daughter Pushpa. He felt a certain level of helplessness and perhaps remorse that he could not be next to his family at such a time. Thoughts on whether his presence in Lahore would have saved Pushpa rushed through his head. Loss of a child is never easy. He had nobody but himself to turn to for solace. It would be many months before he would return to a new India. Lahore, his home for many years, was now a foreign country.

10

The Case that Shook the Crown

In its decision dated 18 March 1948, titled 'High Commissioner for India and High Commissioner for Pakistan v. I.M. Lall'[1] authored by Lord Thankerton, the Privy Council agreed with the findings of the Federal Court that the person being dismissed or reduced must know that the punishment has been proposed for certain acts or omissions on his part and must be told the grounds on which it has been proposed to take such action and must be given a reasonable opportunity of giving show cause, stating why such punishment should not be imposed. These processes were not followed in the present case. Accordingly, the Privy Council eventually found that 'the order of August 10, 1940, purporting to dismiss the respondent from the Indian Civil Service was void and inoperative, and that the respondent remained a member of the Indian Civil Service at the date of the institution of the present action on July 20, 1942'.[2]

The other question, however, was whether damages and arrears of pay could be awarded in the case. On this, the Privy Council reversed the decision of the Federal Court holding

[1]'The High Commissioner For India ... vs I.M. Lall on 18 March, 1948', *Indian Kanoon*, https://tinyurl.com/3vfxp9yr. Accessed on 3 November 2023.

[2]Ibid.

ar. As you probably know, I.M.Lall — of the famous Privy Council
— is being restored to the I.C.S. with the concurrence of the
Punjab Government. We have given a promise to the East Punjab
ment that he would be retained for some time at the Centre in
uitable post. At that time H.M. had in mind a post in the
Ministry concerned with the railway labour which would have been
table in view of Lall's labour activities during his excile
Service. But owing to some difficulties, the possibility
ing that post has receded for the present indefinitely. We
therefore, got a very senior I.C.S. officer and [illegible]
hand without anything to do and there is a problem of
g him.

Correspondence between the Ministry of Home Affairs and the Special Recruitment Board discussing I.M. Lall's reinstatement. I.M. Lall is referred to as I.M. Lall of the 'famous Privy Council case'.
Source: National Archives of India

that public servants are prevented from suing the Crown for their pay. This, the court held, is on the assumption that a public servant's only claim is on the bounty of the Crown and not a contractual debt. The court held that there is an implied condition in every contract between the Crown and a public servant. The condition stipulates that the public servant has no right to their remuneration which can be enforced in a civil court of justice. The only available remedy under their contract lies in an appeal of an official or political kind. The Privy Council did, however, grant costs but did not accede to the costs of his coming to England from India.

According to the Privy Council, the employment of public servants was 'to continue during the pleasure of His Majesty, His Heirs and Successors'. The employment contract is given under the hand of the Secretary of State for India.

Inder Mohan had been dismissed by an order made under

the hand of the Secretary of State for India, and as he was liable to be dismissed at the pleasure of the Crown, he could base no complaint against his dismissal on the contract of service and did not, in fact, do so. He founded his suit on the claim that his dismissal by the Crown from the ICS, of which he was a member, was void and of no effect, as certain mandatory provisions of the Government of India Act, 1935, had not been complied with. The Judicial Committee accepted this claim and thereupon made the declaration that the purported dismissal of the respondent was void and inoperative and he remained a member of the ICS on the date of the institution of his suit.[3]

Impact

This is an important decision for service law jurisprudence in India and has been cited with approval in over 10 Supreme Court decisions subsequently.[4] The decision was a turning point for many reasons. The first being that a subject of the British Empire had won against the Crown. This was the only case with such a result. Never in the history of the Empire had the subject ever prevailed over the Crown. By dismissing him from service, the Crown had violated the basic tenets of service law of not giving him an opportunity to defend himself against the charges levied against him. The decision significantly watered down the existing belief that

---

[3]'Dr. S. B. Dutt vs University Of Delhi on 3 September, 1958', *Indian Kanoon*, https://tinyurl.com/88es6pyh. Accessed on 3 November 2023.

[4]'Khem Chand vs. Union of India, AIR 1958 SC 300'; 'Bhagban Chandra Das v State of Assam', 1971, 1 LLJ 576; *Bhatt (Major U.R.) Versus Union of India*, 1962, 1 LLJ-656; *Ram Chander v UOI*, 1986, 2 LLJ-334.

all civil servants enjoyed their position at the pleasure of the Crown.

The decision formed the very basis of the principles of service law of informing the person of the charges framed against them and giving them an opportunity to show cause and defend themself against the charges. This paved the way for Article 311 of the Constitution of India, a provision dealing with the dismissal, removal or reduction in rank of persons employed in civil capacities under the Union or a state. Article 311 essentially puts restrictions on the pleasure doctrine as discussed in Inder Mohan's case.

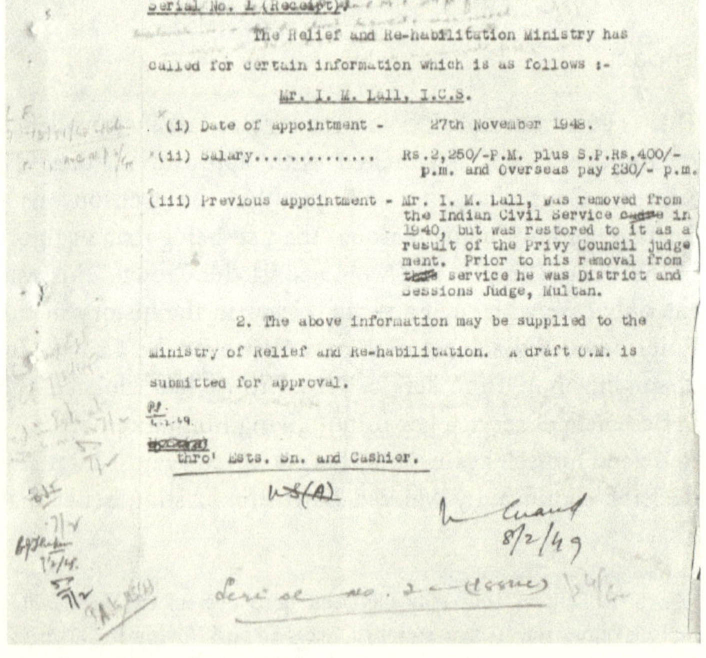

Serial No. 1 (Receipt)

The Relief and Re-habilitation Ministry has called for certain information which is as follows :-

Mr. I. M. Lall, I.C.S.

(i) Date of appointment - 27th November 1948.

(ii) Salary.............. Rs.2,250/-P.M. plus S.P.Rs.400/- p.m. and Overseas pay £30/- p.m.

(iii) Previous appointment - Mr. I. M. Lall, was removed from the Indian Civil Service cadre in 1940, but was restored to it as a result of the Privy Council judgement. Prior to his removal from the service he was District and Sessions Judge, Multan.

2. The above information may be supplied to the Ministry of Relief and Re-habilitation. A draft O.M. is submitted for approval.

thro' Ests. Sn. and Cashier.

8/2/49

Details of I.M. Lall's remuneration after reinstatement to the ICS
Source: National Archives of India

In another case titled 'State of Punjab v I.M. Lall'[5] in which Inder Mohan was represented by D.D. Chawla, C.L. Choudhary and Amar, a Division Bench of the Delhi High Court consisting of V.S. Deshpande and B.C. Mishra narrated the three decisions of the High Court, Federal Court and the Privy Council, and held:

> In penultimate paragraph, the Judicial Committee held that 'removal of I.M. Lall from service was void and a declaration was granted that on the date of the suit that is to say in June, 1942, he remained in service'. This decision was incorporated in an order in Council. In the eye of law, therefore, Mr. Lall never had any break in service and his removal from service having been set aside and declared void and declaration having been granted that hc continued to remain in service, the legal effect was to treat Mr. Lall as in service during the whole period from 1940 to the date of his suit and from the date of the suit till the decision of the Privy Council and, thereafter until legally terminated. During this period, he would naturally be entitled to receive his salary and allowances as if there was no break in service.

Justice had been served. The pleasure of the Crown could not be a curtain behind which the servants of the Crown could undertake capricious or arbitrary actions. The pleasure shall be regulated by rule, said the Privy Council. Inder Mohan was reinstated. His date of re-appointment was 27 November 1948, with a salary of ₹2,250 per month with an additional, ₹400 and overseas pay of £30 per month.

---

[5]'State of Punjab and Anr. vs I.M. Lall on 31 October, 1974', *Indian Kanoon*, https://tinyurl.com/mb8prrau. Accessed on 3 November 2023.

11

Starting Afresh

After the verdict, Inder Mohan returned to India. Much had changed in his absence. One country had become two. His family had been uprooted from Lahore, where they had lived in luxury. They were now refugees. The most heart-wrenching news was that of the loss of his daughter. Victory may have been sweet but at what cost.

Photograph taken on the occasion of the transfer and promotion of P.S. Jain, additional district and sessions judge, Ambala; I.M. Lall seated in the first row (fourth from left)

Source: Lall family albums

After being reinstated, Inder Mohan first became the chairman of the War Pensions Committee under the Ministry of Defence, and thereafter he was transferred to the Rehabilitation Ministry on 17 October 1950, where he was appointed as the chief claims commissioner. A decision in *Hyderabad (Sind) Electric vs Union Of India* (reported as AIR 1959 P&H 199) described his role as an appellate authority above the claims officer. This position required his adjudications on valuation of assets left behind by people in Pakistan and providing them with compensation, inter alia, on the basis of the Displaced Persons (Debts Adjustment) Act, 1951. The decision recorded:

I.M. Lall (sitting second from right) attending an official meeting
Source: Lall family albums

> When India was partitioned in 1947 there was compulsory migration of population from West Pakistan to India and vice versa. The migrants left most of their properties in places where they had resided and carried

on business before the migration. To assist the displaced persons the Parliament placed several statutes on the Statute Book. One of these statutes is the Displaced Persons (Claims) Act. 1950.

Under this Act, authorities were appointed and procedure was laid down for the verification of claims of displaced persons. 'Claim' is defined in the Act as the assertion of a right to the ownership or to any interest in the properties left in West Pakistan. Thus, under the Act, the right of a displaced person to any interest in such property and the value thereof is to be determined by the Claims Officer, who, after registering the claim, has to send the relevant papers to the Central Government.[1]

I.M. Lall (second from left) attending an official meeting
Source: Lall family albums

[1]'The Hyderabad (Sind) Electric ... vs Union of India (Uoi) Etc. on 5 September, 1958', *Indian Kanoon*, https://tinyurl.com/bd2h48mp. Accessed on 3 November 2023.

The order of the claims officer was subject to the revisional powers of the chief claims commissioner. As the claims were settled, this post was abolished, and Inder Mohan went back to the judicial services and became the district and sessions judge in Ambala. He was in Ambala and Shimla during this period, spending 15 days each month in the two locations.

Family Matters

Meanwhile, Inder Mohan's children were pursuing higher education. The eldest, Tilak, was studying in the US. While Inder Mohan had been occupied with the case in India, Tilak had finished his matriculation, at a mere age of 15. In 1940, he had joined the GCUL, the same college where Inder Mohan had completed his Bachelor's. After Inder Mohan had won his case, Tilak expressed a desire to go to England or the US to get an engineering degree. Accordingly, he applied and got admission in the University of California, Berkeley. Having got admission, the next task was to get a US visa. Since Inder Mohan was fairly influential, he was able to arrange the visa from Calcutta.

Amar Raj Lall, Bar-at-Law
Source: Lall family albums

These were still difficult times for travel. Tilak was 23 at that time, and there were no flights or passenger liners. There was a Swedish liner, which was the only passenger ship to the US. Tilak could not get a place aboard, so he decided to take his chance on a US Navy cruise ship, which had a space of 17 bunks reserved for Indians, and he managed

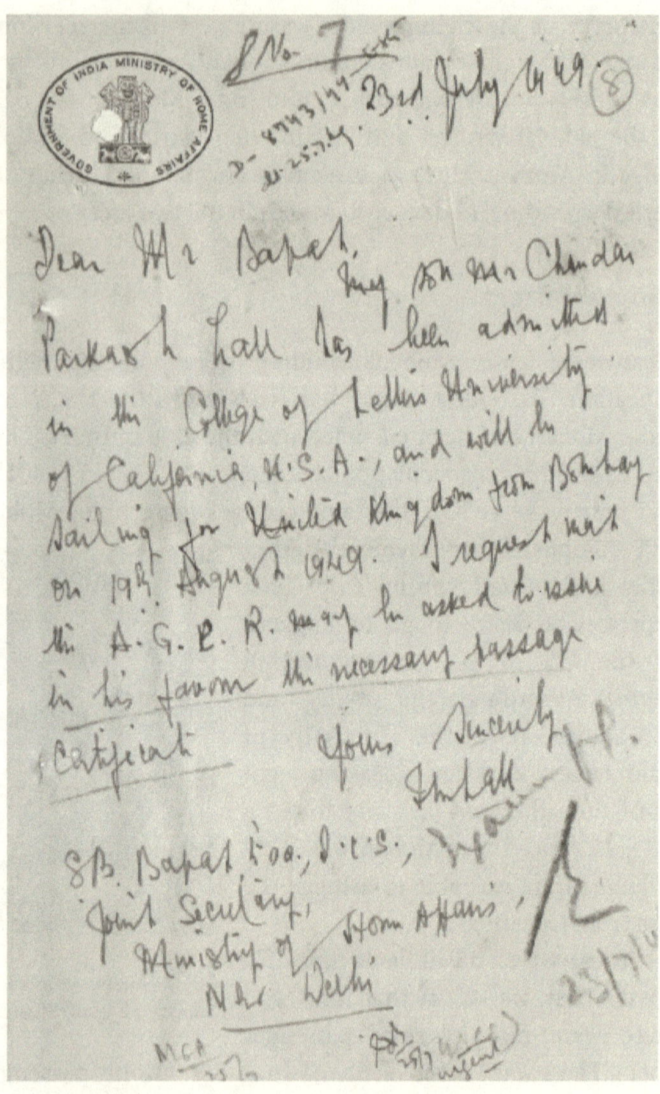

D-8743/49 25.7.49. 23rd July 1949

Dear Mr Bapat,
My son Mr Chander Parkash Lall has been admitted in the College of Letters University of California, U.S.A., and will be sailing for United Kingdom from Bombay on 19th August 1949. I request that the A.G.C.R. may be asked to issue in his favour the necessary passage certificate.

Yours Sincerely
I.M. Lall

S.B. Bapat Esq., I.C.S.,
Joint Secretary,
Ministry of Home Affairs,
New Delhi

I.M. Lall requested passage certification for Chander Parkash Lall to travel to the US
Source: National Archives of India

to get one. Since the ship sailed from Calcutta, Tilak headed there. He reminisced about how the Calcutta harbour was where he got the first taste of America.

The ship had left the Calcutta harbour and gone on to Colombo, through the Bay of Bengal, Arabian Sea, Red Sea, Suez Canal and Mediterranean Sea. It then sailed to Gibraltar and then Atlantic Ocean. It took about a week or so to cross the Atlantic and finally the ship arrived in New York on 26 January 1945. Tilak spent a couple of days in New York in a hotel on 41st Street and thereafter he proceeded to Berkeley hitchhiking his way there.

Extract from letter No.P.515/45/A,dated 16th Sept., 1949, of Indian Embassy, Washington, regarding the total amount paid to Mr.Tilak Raj Lall.
File RL-1(42)/47.

Maintenance Allowance, Sept.1st,1947 to June 30th 1949 -22months @ $ 150.00 per month	$ 3300.00
Tuition Fees	469.50
Book Allowance	100.00
	$ 3869.50

In addition the following payements have been made since that date.

Maintenance allowance,July and August,49 2 months @ $/150.00 per month	300.00
Tuition Fees	185.00
TOTAL XX PAID TO AUGUST 31st,1949..	$ 4354.50

Details of the financial assistance provided to Tilak Raj Lall for his education by the Government of India

Source: National Archives of India

The case had drained the family's financial resources considerably. Inder Mohan applied for a loan for Tilak's education from the government. He was granted a loan against the arrears that had accumulated from the time of his removal from service. He also sent a request for a relaxation of passage regulations for his other two sons: Amar and Chander. Under the Superior Civil Service Rules, a male child of an officer, to whom the regulations apply, was entitled to passage concessions if he was under 12 years of age. This request was, however, denied since they were past that age at the time of the request. In his letter to the ministry, Inder Mohan talked about repaying his loan in two installments:

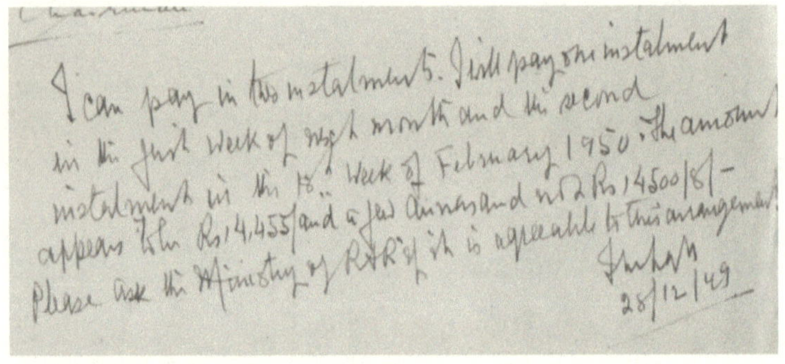

I can pay in two instalments. I will pay one instalment in the first week of next month and the second instalment in the 1st week of February 1950. The amount appears to be Rs 14,455/ and a few annas and not Rs 14500/8/-. Please ask the Ministry of R&R if it is agreeable to this arrangement.
[illegible]
28/12/49

Note explaining the repayment of the loan provided to Tilak Raj Lall
Source: National Archives of India

Despite the odds, Amar became a successful barrister, practising in Delhi, and Chander, an engineer, started work with Boeing in Seattle, US. Tilak joined as an engineer, working in the USA, with McDonnell Douglas and later NASA. Jogi pursued a successful career as Manager Tea Estates in Darjeeling. Savitri and Shiela married Air Force officers, and though Savitri lost her husband early, they lived happy lives.

Retirement and Thereafter

Inder Mohan finally retired in 1957 as the district and sessions judge, Ambala, which was the year Amar got married to Kamla. Post retirement, Inder Mohan started to practise law. He appeared as counsel in many leading cases, including Supreme Court cases, like *Giani Ram v Ramji Lal* (1969), *Harbans Singh v the State of Punjab* (1962), *Krishan Lal Dhawan v the Delhi Administration* (1963). He also appeared in criminal cases, such as '*Masalti v the State of Uttar Pradesh* (1964, 1965) and *Banarsi Das Ahluwalia v the Chief Controlling Revenue Authority of India*' (1968).

Left to right: I.M. Lall, Amar Lall and Dropadi
Source: Lall family albums

Inder Mohan also saw matters requiring interpretation of the Constitution, such as *Moti Ram Deka v General Manager, North East Frontier Railway* (1964), which involved interpretation of Articles 309, 310 and 311 of the Constitution relating to a public servant and tenure of service and termination, issues which he was personally very familiar with. Other service law-related matters included the case of *Roshan Lal Tandon v Union of India* (1968), which involved an interpretation of Articles 14, 16 and 32 of the Constitution, relating to the denial of equal treatment to skilled artisans. *Sajjan Singh v State of Punjab* (1964) was a case relating to illegal gratification under the Prevention of Corruption Act, wherein Inder Lall appeared along with B.N. Kirpal, who eventually went on to become the Chief Justice of India.

12

I.M. Lall, Chief Claims Commissioner: The Final Word

It was 4 September 1952. On the lawns of the Imperial Hotel on Janpath in Delhi, Inder Mohan Lall, ICS, chief claims commissioner, gave his valedictory speech, bidding farewell to the outgoing claims officers who worked under him. His wife, Dropadi, and daughter, Shiela, the only two women in the audience, were listening. Shiela, all dressed up for the occasion, glowed with pride on hearing her father. The *pallu* of Dropadi's saree covered her head, and her eyes looked down, thus camouflaging the pride she felt for her husband.

The hotel itself stood tall on Janpath, or what used to be Queensway under the British. The rooms of the hotel had been witness to one of the initial meetings between Mahatma Gandhi, Lord Mountbatten, Pandit Nehru and Muhammed Ali Jinnah, where the men discussed the partition of India and the formation of Pakistan. The white walls of the hotel, held by the giant pillars of British architecture, tell a story of how the meeting was a cordial one under congenial conditions. Inder Mohan, the 6-ft plus giant of a man, stood on the same veranda with the backdrop of the large circular pillars. Here was a man who had single-handedly fought the might of the British Empire. He did not bow to the whims of the Crown or the pleasure of His Majesty.

A part of his speech was about his past: 'I was appointed at the pleasure of His Majesty, but it took a large part of my professional life to understand and help define that pleasure. I am happy to see that my struggle paved the way for future generations, for they shall not be burdened by its ire, but its pure pleasure. Inder Mohan hailed the judiciary, an institution he had been an integral part of. In doing so, he proved himself to be the true protector of the rule of law and a champion for those who had been wronged.'

Tea party organized to bid farewell to the outgoing claims officer and to meet I.M. Lall, ICS chief claims commissioner (standing), on 4 September 1952, at Hotel Imperial, Janpath, New Delhi. His wife, Dropadi (in white saree), and daughter Shiela (extreme left) can also be seen in the picture.
Source: Lall family albums

Afterword

In this riveting book, Chander M. Lall talked about the struggles of his grandfather against the British rule, being a part of the prestigious Indian Civil Services (ICS), and ignited the thought about similar struggles and contributions of numerous other known and unknown Indian men and women. The Indian freedom movement can be categorized as one which was largely peaceful despite the participation of people from all strata of society.

The story of Inder Mohan Lall, who retired as the district and sessions judge, Ambala, in 1957, is one such telling tale of a young and ambitious boy who hailed from a small village of Mianwali in present-day Pakistan. He not only received a law degree but also went on to serve in the Indian contingent sent to Mesopotamia by England during the First World War. The political implications of the contributions made by over a million Indian soldiers who fought in the war and the sacrifice by thousands who perished were significant for India in terms of the freedom struggle. I.M. Lall was one such braveheart who, despite having secured a prestigious law degree, chose to be a part of the war efforts.

Having survived the war where a large portion of the Indian contingent perished, Lall went on to qualify for the ICS in 1922. He displayed fearless passion towards preserving the ruins of the monastic complex and Gandhara statues as Indian heritage, while the British considered all of India as their personal property. In this light, it was fitting when Shashi Tharoor said at the Oxford Union Debate: 'The sun never set on the British empire because even God couldn't trust the

Englishman in the dark.'[1] It was Lall's support to Nicholas Roerich towards the preservation of this heritage that ruffled the feathers and broke loose the ire of the mighty Crown.

His legal battle against the Crown for his wrongful dismissal from the ICS is indeed inspiring. The book has beautifully captured the journey, right from the District Court up to the Privy Council. Each time, he won against the Crown and established a fundamental principle of service law, which remains good law till date. This book also delves into the circumstances in which the life of I.M. Lall was set and enlightens the reader about some of the most important historical events that India witnessed during its freedom struggle. The plight of the people who lost their lives during Partition has been focussed upon, and the sorrowful narration of the same sends a chill down the spine even decades later. It is in this backdrop that Lall had to travel to England, leaving behind his family during those turbulent times, to argue his case before the Privy Council himself, if necessary, as no lawyer in England had the courage to take up his case against the Crown. His resolve to prove his case against all odds and the wherewithal of the Crown is a fitting example of the old saying: 'Perseverance conquers all!'

This book is an apt tribute to the man with a stature so high that it brought down the mighty Crown to its knees, as he became the only subject to have ever won a case against them. The book will not only be enjoyed and cherished by all but also inspire them to persevere against all odds and believe in the power of truth.

—Justice Sanjay Kishan Kaul
Judge, Supreme Court of India

---

[1]Tharoor, Shashi, *An Era of Darkness: The British Empire in India*, Aleph Book Company, 2016.

Acknowledgements

I dedicate this book to my father, Amar Raj Lall, barrister-at-law. But for his storytelling abilities and narratives of the past, this book would never have been written. He made them so interesting that even a young boy, which is what I was in the good old days, could not but get enthralled. Such was his recountal, that despite my poor memory retention, I was able to recapitulate large portions of it. Unfortunately, I could not ask the right questions at the right time and had to therefore fall back on the Internet for many details.

I also dedicate this book to my mother, Kamla, and my brother, Anil (and his wife Manju), who gave me some very critical trigger points, and I am thankful for that. I could not imagine why the British Raj, known for its righteousness, would be so uncharitable towards my grandfather. The Roerich episode seemed to provide some answers. My mother was also able to pull out some very precious photographs, which can be found in this book.

My memory banks were also augmented by the recordings made by our family friend Julie Winokur, a journalist and a film-maker from San Francisco. Julie spent hours with my father recording his memories. She was nice enough to pull these recordings out of her closets, have them digitized and share them with me.

I am also thankful to my cousins Neal, Kris and Anne in Seattle for making recordings of their father (my namesake

Chander P. Lall) narrating his adventures. These were shared with me and greatly helped me piece together one part of the story. My cousin Cheri in Los Angeles gave me one of the most cherished pictures from her father, Tilak's, collection.

This book is also dedicated to my entire family, to whom this story must be told and recounted. To my niece, Shivani, to whom her *nanu* (Amar), was her favourite person on Earth. Of course, I am also thankful to my sister-in-law Simran for carefully proofreading the book despite (or maybe because of) a plastered leg.

Thanks to my friend Kirti Sethi for her invaluable suggestions; to my wife, who thought I was working, earning the bucks, whereas I was spending hours researching and writing this book; to my children, Ishan and Utsav, both having pursued a legal education.

I also dedicate this book to the legal fraternity, as it is an important historical account of how one important provision of the Constitution of India metamorphosed.

Of course, a final dedication to Samrata Salwan Diwan and her team at Family Fables for their research, edits and copy edits. But for her persistence and patience, and of course her indefatigable talent, this beautiful publication would never have materialized.

Bibliography

Andreyev, Alexandre, *Soviet Russia and Tibet: The Debacle of Secret Diplomacy, 1918–1930s*, Brill, Boston, 2003.

Burra, Arudra, 'The Indian Civil Service and the Raj: 1919–1950', *SSRN*, 7 May 2012, https://tinyurl.com/8bs8m2y2.

Bakaya, Ravi M., and Pandit Pearay Mohan, *The Punjab 'Rebellion' of 1919 and How It Was Suppressed: An Account of the Punjab Disorders and the Working of Martial Law*, Gyan Publishing House, 1999.

Cadell, Patrick, 'The Raising of the Indian Army', *Journal of the Society for Army Historical Research*, Vol. 34, No. 139, 1956.

Catherwood, Christopher, *The Battles of World War I: Everything You Need to Know*, Allison & Busby, United Kingdom, 2014.

'Gandhi and Civil Disobedience', *Teach Democracy*,
https://tinyurl.com/2xs7nk9p.

Dalrymple, William, 'The Great Divide', The New Yorker, 22 June 2015, https://tinyurl.com/2p8v76kn.

Desai, Kishwar, *Jallianwala Bagh, 1919: The Real Story*, Westland Limited, 2019.

Dewey, Clive, *Anglo-Indian Attitudes: Mind of the Indian Civil Service*, Bloomsbury, United Kingdom, 1993.

Doctor, Vikram, 'General Dyer: The Man behind the Jallianwala Bagh Massacre', *The Economic Times*, 14 April 2019, https://tinyurl.com/sahdm79z. Accessed on 24 July 2023.

Garrett, H. L. O, and Abdul Hamid, *A History of Government College Lahore*, Ripon Print Press, Lahore, 1964.

Habib, Irfan, 'Jallianwala Bagh Massacre: The First Wave of Mass

Struggle and Its Aftermath, 1919–26', *Social Scientist*, Vol. 47, No. 5/6, 2019, pp. 3–8.

Hajari, Nisid, *Midnight's Furies: The Deadly Legacy of India's Partition*, Penguin Books Limited, India, 2016.

Bhavnani, J.K., 'Legal Education in India', *Journal of Indian Law Institute*, Vol. 4, No. 2, 1962, pp. 167–90.

Kaushik, R.K., 'Indian Civil Service: Steel Frame of the British', The *Times of India*, 23 April 2018, https://tinyurl.com/y8bacv85.

Kaushik, R.K., 'Tracing the History of Civil Services Recruitment', *The Tribune*, 13 May 2008, https://tinyurl.com/2rf6b63w.

Latter, Edwin, 'The Indian Army in Mesopotamia 1914–1918, Part 2', *Journal of the Society for Army Historical Research*, Vol. 72, 1994, pp. 168–9, 172–3.

Woodruff, Philip. *The Men Who Ruled India: The Founders*, J. Cape, United Kingdom, 1953.

Saigal, D.D., *Footprints on Sand: An Autobiography*, Yash Publications, India, 2014.

Gonsalves, Trijita, 'From ICS to IAS: A Historical Review of the Civil Services in India', *ResearchGate*, September 2019, https://tinyurl.com/2z8bzhxv.

'Siege and Surrender of Kut-el-Amara: Official Report of General Sir Percy Lake', 1916, *Current History (1916-1940)*, Vol. 5, No. 3, 1916, pp. 545–49.

Singh, Kavita, '"Mountain Muse"–An Exploration to Human Consciousness and Eternity', *Gyankosh: An Interdisciplinary E-Journal*, Vol. 1, 2018, https://tinyurl.com/3uzx97zd.

Singh, Khushwant, *Punjab, Punjabis and Punjabiyat: Reflections on a Land and Its People*, Aleph Book Company, India, 2018.

Vohra, Ranbir, *Making of India: A Historical Survey*, M.E. Sharpe, 2001.

www.ingramcontent.com/pod-product-compliance
Lightning Source LLC
La Vergne TN
LVHW090520110826
845146LV00003B/937

* 9 7 8 9 3 5 7 0 2 7 5 1 9 *